scandinavian country

scandinavian country

MAGNUS ENGLUND & CHRYSTINA SCHMIDT

photography by Paul Ryan

RYLAND
PETERS
& SMALL

LONDON NEW YORK

First published in the UK in 2007
by Ryland Peters & Small
20–21 Jockey's Fields
London WC1R 4BW
www.rylandpeters.com

10 9 8 7 6 5 4 3 2 1

ISBN: 978-1-84597-352-0

A CIP record from this book is
available from the British Library.

Printed and bound in China.

Senior designer **Paul Tilby**
Senior editor **Henrietta Heald**
Location research **Chrystina Schmidt**
and **Jess Walton**
Production manager **Patricia Harrington**
Publishing director **Alison Starling**

contents

introduction

This book celebrates the Scandinavians' love of living in the countryside, be it in a traditional house or in an ultra-modern architect-designed creation. The featured homes vary according to their locations, but their owners have one thing in common: a need to be close to nature and the elements, to be able to see the seasons shift in a way impossible in the city. Perhaps they long for a bygone, less complicated era when the only sound was the rustling of the leaves in the trees. Living close to nature is a luxury for many people in the modern world, but it remains part of what it means to be a true Scandinavian.

Scandinavia is a vast area encompassing great variations. Sweden is the largest country in the region and the fourth largest in Europe. Depending on how you see it, Denmark is either the smallest Scandinavian country or the largest of all; it consists of Denmark proper, the Faroes and the great landmass of Greenland. Denmark itself is flat, while both Norway and Sweden have high mountains in the north. Finland is less mountainous but has the highest number of lakes, estimated at 190,000. There are also numerous islands that make up the archipelago between Finland and Sweden; the exact figure depends on the definition of 'island' – estimates vary between 20,000 and 50,000. As this book shows, a Scandinavian country home is rarely far from water.

Scandinavia was industrialized later than its neighbours further south, so agriculture was the main occupation until the early 20th century. This means that, only a couple of generations ago, most people lived on the land, and modern Scandinavians have often kept in touch with the areas they came from. Many have inherited old farmhouses that now make popular rural retreats. This also influences the style of food, with wild food such as mushrooms, berries and fresh fish predominating. The Sámi people of northern Scandinavia make a living from herding reindeer, and the autumn elk-hunting season is a favourite pastime even for city-dwellers.

THE **ELEMENTS**

OPPOSITE, ABOVE LEFT **A traditional elegant manor house with a mature landscaped garden is the perfect retreat for many Scandinavians.**

OPPOSITE, ABOVE RIGHT **Windows, doors and door furniture are often discarded from older buildings. To preserve them is to preserve the soul of the house.**

OPPOSITE, BELOW AND INSET **It would be difficult to get closer to nature than this, without sleeping outside under the stars. The front-door handle is a tree root, cleverly positioned to follow the diagonal door planks. Such handles were common in the early 19th century.**

ABOVE RIGHT **Following the advent of longer holidays in 1950s Scandinavia, small, affordable and architecturally interesting houses sprang up along coasts and lakes.**

RIGHT **Old-style building methods can be used in new houses like this one. As in modernist homes, the construction technique is on show.**

FAR RIGHT **The timber industry is a major business in Sweden and Finland, competing with industrial giants such as Nokia and Ericsson. It is no surprise that timber houses are still popular.**

architectural styles

One striking feature about travelling in Scandinavia is that the further north you go, the fewer people you see. Another is the vast forests, which you can drive through for hours. In the past, this meant that people from different areas seldom met, and building styles evolved in local clusters in response to landscape and climate, with little outside influence.

While city architecture has lost this link with nature, it is still very noticeable in the countryside. For example, the Danes are blessed with a milder climate than others in the region. Modern Danish houses are often boxlike structures with large windows and flat roofs, which would not be ideal in areas of arctic temperatures and heavy snowfall. Brick and tiles are much more common in Denmark than in the timber-rich north, a feature also seen in southern Sweden.

Swedes are used to having the forest nearby, and many of their houses are built in woodland clearings or beside small lakes. The most conspicuous feature of these houses is their red-painted wooden façades. The paint was a by-product of the large copper mine in Falun; originally regarded as an affordable and durable means of protecting timber against water damage, it has remained popular.

ABOVE AND ABOVE LEFT **A house that blends in with the landscape, rather than dominating it, is a relatively new idea, but it suits today's strict building regulations. In these examples, the trees shield parts of the houses while adding to the overall architectural effect. The natural colours framing the houses change with the seasons.**

LEFT AND FAR LEFT **Scandinavians share their fondness for wood and other natural materials with many cultures around the world, not least the Japanese, whose traditional building styles also use intricate wall constructions.**

OPPOSITE, ABOVE AND BELOW **Boxlike structures are influenced partly by modernist architecture in warmer climates and partly by the economical reality of the 1950s and 1960s, when resources were scarce. Today's box-shaped house is more about harmonizing with nature and letting the surrounding landscape make the big gestures.**

Finland has the youngest housing stock in Europe, partly because many people have left northern and central Finland to move south to the Helsinki area, and have built new homes. It also stems from the Second World War. When the German army retreated north into Norway, it destroyed everything in its way, so that hardly any prewar buildings remain in northern Finland. Modern country houses, almost always including a sauna, are therefore the Finnish norm.

The architecture of Norway, the most mountainous region of Scandinavia, has been shaped by local terrain and the country's long-established seafaring tradition. Styles have evolved from the need to build on awkward sites, with houses apparently clinging to rocks and steep valleys.

a matter of **materials**

Scandinavia covers a huge distance from north to south, embracing several environmental zones; some 15 per cent of Sweden lies inside the Arctic Circle, while in the case of Finland and Norway it is almost 50 per cent. Denmark and southern Sweden are much more like mainland Europe, with flat plains and fields rather than forests dominating the scene. These regional differences have influenced buildings;

houses were historically built from local materials, and the materials available in southern Scandinavia were distinct from those in the north. Oak and beech, for example, do not grow further north than central Scandinavia. Temperature differences call for different types of heating and insulation; temperatures of −45°C are common in the north while the south gets scarcely any snow. Alvar Aalto's Finlandia Hall in Helsinki (built 1967–72) illustrates the kind of problem that can arise. Aalto chose Italian Carrara marble for the façade, forcing the City of Helsinki to replace the warped stones

THIS PAGE **In southern Scandinavia people have traditionally made a living from the land, but northerners survived in a much more hostile environment. However, although the ground was rocky and difficult to harvest, timber was abundant. The birch tree grows even in the far north of Scandinavia, and is still used for furniture and house-building as well as for fuel. Wood is also a very good insulator, superior to many man-made materials, and highly suitable for houses in cold climates. One benefit of the rocky ground – the remains of deposits from the ice ages – is the many drystone walls still found across Scandinavia. They are testament to generations of hard work.**

OPPOSITE **Old building techniques relied on what was easily available, and in northern Scandinavia this was timber. While the joinery of this table might look crude, it has an inner beauty that could never be matched by a machine-made piece. This is a disappearing skill, making the table unique.**

RIGHT AND BELOW **Wood joinery is a difficult skill to master. It is not just a matter of slotting the pieces together to meet a set of static conditions; how the wood will react to changing levels of temperature and humidity must also be taken into account, and in Scandinavia the highs and lows can be extreme. Still, a well-made wooden joint has a certain beauty that testifies to the skill and care that contributed to its creation. Without skirting boards and fillers to hide mistakes, precision is paramount.**

OPPOSITE **Concrete and brick are entirely different from wood, but can be as unforgiving in that they show the true nature of the construction. Used in its raw form, concrete can look as natural as wood. When combined with steel and timber, it takes on an austere but trustworthy appearance. Like large areas of glass, it makes its presence felt without being obtrusive. This approach to the use of materials is entirely different from the south European attitude.**

at huge cost in 1999. Had Aalto not been such an iconic architect, they would have been replaced by granite. Cold has already started to warp the marble tiles again.

Modern Danish and Finnish houses show the regional differences. The Danes experiment with concrete, brick, steel and glass while the Finns, despite also building in a modern style, are more loyal to traditional timber and stone. Finnish architects favour intricate timber constructions and joints, while the Danes prefer straight surfaces and undisturbed lines. However, there is a distinct move towards a better understanding of traditional building materials all across the region. The 1960s and 1970s was probably the low point of traditional building materials, and many house owners now regret the cheap and quick choices they made then.

Large sliding doors blur the border between inside and out, and the continuation of the wooden box from the terrace into the house underlines this feeling. Like the house itself, the black rattan chairs and the white dining table are by Danish designers. Using cacti to give a defiant impression of warmer climates has been a favourite ploy of Scandinavian designers since the 1930s.

outdoor **living**

There is a prevailing myth that Scandinavia is cold. In fact, summers are as warm as in any other northern European country, with temperatures regulated by the Gulf Stream that brings warm water past its shores. However, the dream of living outdoors means having the Norse gods of weather on your side, which can sometimes call for a lot of praying. The summer lasts only from June to August, and even if the summer days can be very warm, sunshine is not always guaranteed. Then there are the insects to battle with; flies might not be a nuisance unless you are close to a farm, but the mosquitoes are a formidable force to be reckoned with.

THIS PICTURE **The Danish summer sky is reflected in the glass of the house. The outdoor sink and grill move food preparation closer to nature and to the vegetables in the garden nearby. Within minutes of being picked and rinsed, the vegetables can be served on the outdoor table, with diners safe in the knowledge that they are genuinely organic and free from any pesticides.**

LEFT AND OPPOSITE **Summers may be short, but the northern latitude provides one particular advantage: the sun sets only fleetingly. Late at night there is a glow created by the sun positioned just below the horizon, and the glow appears again in the early morning. The long sunlit evenings are perfect for dining in the open air.**

BELOW **Sailing and the sea have been an integral part of life in Scandinavia since before the time of the Vikings. The Baltic and the Kattegat – the part of the Atlantic west of Scandinavia – are awash with white sails in summer. For many, the interior of a sailing boat is their favourite country house. Winter tasks include cleaning and repainting the boats in preparation for the following summer.**

The development of country houses with running water, electricity and modern appliances has made outdoor living much easier than it used to be, but it has also removed the sense of being really close to nature. The Finns in particular pride themselves on living the wild life, sometimes laughing at their Scandinavian neighbours for rigging up their country homes with satellite TV, fixed telephone lines and plumbing.

The art of outdoor living includes the whole business of food preparation. It often starts by rowing out at night in a small boat to lay the nets, getting up early the next morning to bring in the catch, then rowing back to shore and hanging the nets, followed by the time-consuming task of disentangling them from seaweed, sticks and leaves. After a quick dip in the sea or lake, it is time to grill or smoke the fish over a wood fire. It is then eaten with fresh potato, crispbread and a simple salad, washed down by a cold local beer and a shot of vodka.

ABOVE **The woollen rya rug, out of fashion since the 1960s, is making a comeback. Originally intended to be laid on wooden floors, the rya also works well as a wall decoration. Old ryas by renowned Scandinavian weavers and designers are becoming increasingly valuable.**

ABOVE RIGHT, SMALL PICTURES **Antti Nurmesniemi made his sauna stool in the 1950s for the Palace hotel, Helsinki. To anyone not used to saunas, it may look like a toilet seat with legs, but it makes perfect functional sense to anyone in a steamy 38°C environment. The coffee table by NollaNolla supports a wicker basket. A good throw is required for late summer nights.**

RIGHT **The manufacture of bentwood furniture was a 1930s Scandinavian reaction to the bent-steel furniture of the Bauhaus school in Germany. How could the modernist style be adapted to the Scandinavian wooden reality? Alvar Aalto was a pioneer in the field, developing methods with the Korhonen factory in Finland.**

furniture and **textiles**

In a city flat, you may feel the need to furnish to impress friends and colleagues; in the country, you can give freer rein to your personal choice. There is also likely to be more room for furniture that combines comfort and function, and for pieces that are expected to remain there year after year – to be rediscovered like old friends when you return.

Scandinavian country furniture and textiles are often very adaptable, at ease outdoors as well as indoors, so that there is no reservation about dragging chairs and tables outside on a sunny day, or snuggling up in a warm throw in response to a sudden change in wind direction. Country furniture should require minimum maintenance, capable of surviving proximity to dirty shoes and wet clothes.

Nowhere are the regional differences in Scandinavian taste more apparent than in the choice of country furniture and textiles. The Finns often go for a style that is rustic but functional, incorporating inherited pieces of kitchenware and seating to create an individual mix. They shun things that are too new, since age is unimportant; the real action is outdoors in any case. The Norwegians take much the same pragmatic attitude. By contrast, in new Danish and Swedish country homes, interiors are a priority. If furniture is

ABOVE LEFT **Using the attic as a living area is only possible with modern central heating. In old buildings the attic was seldom used for anything but storage; its most common feature would probably have been wasps' nests, so it is apt that this Japanese paper lamp was inspired by a wasps' nest. The crisscross design on the window shows that the owner liked intricate constructions – and double-glazing.**

ABOVE **The Lamino chair by Yngve Ekström, designed in 1955 for his own company Swedese, is a real Swedish classic, which was recently awarded a prize as the most popular Swedish design of the 20th century. While it looks sturdy enough, it is delivered flat-packed and predates the creations of Ingvar Kamprad, the founder of IKEA, who hails from Småland, the same region of Sweden as Ekström.**

antique, then it really is antique, not just some old leftover without provenance. This even goes for outdoor pieces, which are often new and modern. The Finns and Norwegians, on the other hand, are as likely to use nearby rocks and trees as outdoor furniture.

Textiles can be traditional or even childish, reminiscent of summers or winters long ago. Curtains are mainly required to exclude the Scandinavian midnight sun; the further north you go, the longer the summer nights. The winter nights, by contrast, are pitch black, even if the whiteness of the snow reflects the moonlight and stars more than you would expect.

THIS PAGE **The Hoop chair by Hans J. Wegner looks like it was designed in the 1950s, yet this master of Danish furniture design created it in the 1980s. Wegner's career stretches from the early 1950s; his most popular and well-known chair is the Wishbone (or Y chair, as it is known in Scandinavia) from 1950. The Hoop chair, made by PP Møbler in Denmark, is one of Wegner's most complex designs; the frame must be moistened and forced into shape by hand before the strings are attached.**

OPPOSITE, ABOVE **In the 18th century, French influence on Scandinavian style was partly politically driven; the Scandinavian courts favoured France over Germany and Britain. The fashion of that time called for furniture to be placed against the walls rather than in the middle of the room, so sofa seating was very popular.**

OPPOSITE, BELOW **While continental Europe in the 19th century saw a connection between the naked legs of chairs and the naked legs of women, Scandinavia never really encountered such moral problems. The focus was on the intricate construction of the seat backs rather than on covering the legs.**

THE **HOUSES**

TRADITIONAL
COUNTRY

A traditional Scandinavian country home can mean anything from a simple farmstead to a Viking-inspired house built in the nationalist romantic era of the late 19th century. It can also mean a modern building that incorporates old features such as thatching or timbering. Common to all these homes is the fact that they use construction techniques that have either been generally forgotten or are considered too inefficient for modern living, but that nevertheless result in beautiful homes.

OPPOSITE **The old inn was built some time around 1750, right by the water, on a reclaimed seabed. The present owners are keen sailors and they keep several boats. There are also boats available for making deep-sea fishing expeditions further out in the Atlantic Ocean.**

RIGHT **The house is so close to the water that, when the owners open a hatch in the floor, they can see crabs crawling underneath.**

NORWEGIAN **WOOD**

Far out in the Atlantic Ocean coast lies a Norwegian timber house that used to be deserted in summer but busy in winter, on account of the fishing calendar. These days, the situation is reversed, with an abundance of summer visitors, but inside the building time has stood still.

TOP RIGHT **The old bell recalls the time when the house was an inn; it would be rung each day to announce that dinner was ready.**

ABOVE RIGHT **The 19th-century carpenter's skill is displayed in the finely wrought entrance door.**

Brekkestø is a small village on the southern coast of Norway, in a region known as Sørlandet (the South Land). Brekkestø is a part of the municipality of Lillesand, in the county of Aust-Agder. These might sound like geographical references from *The Lord of the Rings*, but then J. R. R. Tolkien was an expert on Scandinavian languages, and in particular old Norwegian and Icelandic.

Fishing and sailing are still important industries in Norway, and the history of Brekkestø is closely connected with these activities. The Norwegian coast is made up of long fjords, cutting deep into the country. During winter, these fjords freeze over, and it was therefore essential for the old seafarers to base their fleets as far out into the ice-free ocean as possible so that they would be in a position to set sail early each spring. Villages with harbours were located on the extremities of the coast, and Brekkestø is one of those villages. In summer, the ships would be at sea, and Brekkestø would be empty of menfolk, but in winter the village would become a veritable hive of activity. Ropemakers, carpenters, smiths and sailmakers repaired and re-equipped the ships

RIGHT **The flags from Norwegian merchant vessels that have been used to decorate the entrance to the house are a reminder of the long tradition of maritime activity in Brekkestø. The staircase is as steep as on any ship. The end of the staircase is decorated with a dolphin, a species that is found in the seas nearby.**

FAR RIGHT **The central core of the house is clad in raw timber that has been painted, while the rooms leading off it have plastered walls. The house seems to be full of pieces of furniture that have been there for years, but the reality is different; old fishing houses often relied on foreign imports.**

BELOW **When the tide is high, the water line reaches right up to the front of the house. The water retreats after a few hours, and it seems as if the salt water actually impregnates the timber, making it rock hard.**

in the harbour in preparation for the following spring. They all needed lodging, and the village inn was the establishment that provided it. The house featured in these pages was that same inn.

The village of Brekkestø is spread over several rocky islands. Its nearest town is Lillesand, accessible by a network of roads and bridges. Many of the homes built around Brekkestø's compact harbour are white wooden cottages with red-tiled roofs, typical of the area, giving the place a very quaint impression. Early 20th-century writers and painters such as Christian Krohg, Nils Kjær and Gabriel Scott retreated to Brekkestø in search of inspiration during the quiet summers. That said, nowadays the small village is often crowded

with tourists during the peak summer months, while in winter the village is virtually deserted − precisely the opposite of the situation that prevailed 100 or even 50 years ago.

The old inn was built some time around 1750; no one knows the date or year exactly. The style is similar to what was constructed in New England at the same time. It is right next to the water, built on old seabed that has been reclaimed by filling it up with rocks and stones. This may have been done in order to acquire the land cheaply, or to avoid having to seek building permission, but these are only theories. What is sure is that the house is so close to the water that, when the owners open a

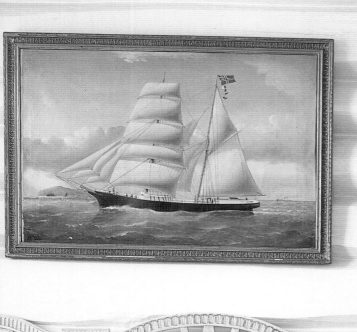

THIS PAGE **The angel was a motif often seen in old sailing ships; when a ship far out at sea was lashed by ferocious storms, prayers frequently represented the sailors' last hope of salvation. Norwegian merchant vessels such as the one in the painting were already crossing the oceans in the early 18th century, just as they do today. Even the Antarctic was within their reach, as the Norwegian names given to many remote islands tell.**

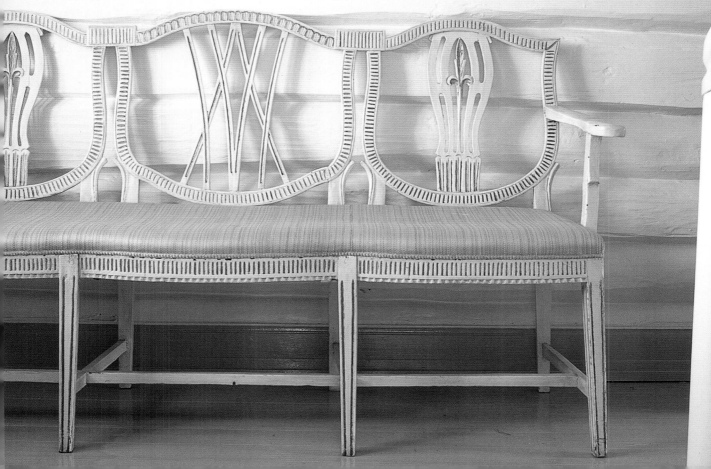

≪≪ THE PRESENT OWNERS ARE KEEN SAILORS AND KEEP SEVERAL BOATS. THEY USE THE HOUSE FROM SPRING UNTIL OCTOBER, WHICH IS ALSO THE START OF THE LOBSTER-FISHING SEASON. ≫≫

ABOVE LEFT **This classic writing desk has its roots in 19th-century Denmark. The high-back chair is probably English and brought to Norway in a Norwegian ship.**

BELOW LEFT **The extension table in Gustavian style in the dining room is early 20th century; it may be made up of several unrelated parts that have been used together.**

ABOVE **The sofa by the window is Danish and from the 18th century. The ship model on the wall, known as a half-model, was common in the mid-19th century. It holds a miniature ship cut in half, and then glued onto the bottom of the box. The chest of drawers beneath is also Danish, possibly dating from the late 17th century.**

hatch in the floor, they can see crabs crawling underneath. When the tide is high – and it is very high every other year – the water reaches right up to the front door of the house. With a new house made from modern building materials, this would be a disaster, but in this case it does not seem to matter. The water retreats after a few hours anyway, and it seems as if the salt impregnates the timber, making it rock hard.

The present occupiers have owned the house for some 50 years, and were among the first summer visitors to buy a house in Brekkestø rather than simply lodging with the village's permanent inhabitants. The house appears to be filled with pieces of furniture that have been there since the house was built, but the reality is quite different. The seamen of 100 or 200 years ago often brought their furniture from abroad, from Victorian Britain or imperial Germany. The style of that time was dark and heavy, far from the type of furniture featured

LEFT **The seamen of a century or more ago frequently brought back with them furniture found during their travels abroad, in Britain or Germany, for example. The style of that time was dark and heavy. Today the house is full of old pieces, but most of them are from Norway or Denmark, in the much lighter 18th-century Gustavian style, which remains popular in Scandinavia.**

RIGHT **The large bed dates from the early 20th century. Opposite it has been hung a classic Union mirror, celebrating the union of Sweden and Norway, which lasted from 1814 until 1905.**

BELOW **The harbour bed outside the house holds artefacts derived from 400 years of maritime activity. It is not unusual to come across, for example, old bottles, chalk pipes, glass floats and other relics. Some of these objects have made their way into the house as decorations.**

≪ THE NORWEGIAN COAST IS MADE UP OF LONG FJORDS THAT FREEZE OVER IN WINTER. IT WAS THEREFORE ESSENTIAL FOR THE OLD SEAFARERS TO BASE THEIR FLEETS AS FAR OUT INTO THE ICE-FREE OCEAN AS POSSIBLE SO THEY COULD SET SAIL EARLY EACH SPRING. ≫

today. The current furniture is also old, but most of it comes from Norway or Denmark and is in a much lighter style. The sandy shore outside the house is a repository of artefacts that bear witness to 400 years of activity, some of which have made their way into the house as decorative objects. Another reminder of the working life at sea are the flags from Norwegian merchant vessels.

The present owners are keen sailors and keep several boats. They generally use the house from April until October; while the autumn is cold and windy, it is also the start of the lobster-fishing season – which many might regard as a good reason to stay behind. Fish is the main diet in Brekkestø, and people travel there from far and wide to buy fresh fish, eat at the small restaurants or try their own luck at fishing. There are even boats available to rent or join for deep-sea fishing further out in the Atlantic Ocean.

DANISH **THATCH**

Situated on the island of Rømø in Denmark, this modern house incorporates the ancient technique of thatching, in this case with reed. The architects behind it – Schmidt Hammer Lassen – are best known for their Black Diamond building on the waterfront in Copenhagen, which forms part of the Danish Royal Library complex.

LEFT AND BELOW **The choice of a thatched roof in what is essentially a modern building is bold but works surprisingly well. The roof lights save the inside from a lack of sunshine and are built in uncompromisingly contemporary style, while the façade, with its screenlike structure, shows an obvious Japanese influence.**

OPPOSITE **In old Scandinavia, thatched roofs were a building feature that was virtually unique to Denmark, spilling over only into the former Danish province of Skåne in southern Sweden. The climate further north simply would not support the growth of the required material, so turf was used instead.**

Thatched roofs were traditionally made from rye grass, except in the more fertile parts of Denmark, where oat grass was used instead. In general, reed was used only in fishing communities where rye or oat grass was not a commonly available by-product of agriculture. It is appropriate, then, that this reed-thatched house is located on the coast. It stands on a high point of Rømø island, looking east to Jutland across the water. There are other, older thatched houses on Rømø, further down the coast, but this contemporary building differs markedly from its older neighbours in the style of its construction, which permits the penetration of light from every angle.

The abundance of light is the first quality that the owners, Jette Friis and Lars Hansen, praise when talking about their home; in spite of its dark and heavy roof, there is light in every corner. The design also gives them an uninterrupted view of nature. Like an enormous birdwatchers' hide, it allows them to watch the wildlife all around them every day of the year. Rømø is renowned for its bird population and a powerful set of binoculars is an indispensable part of the household equipment.

Rømø is almost 10 km from the mainland of Denmark, at the rim of the North Sea, and has about 850 permanent residents. It evolved from a sandbank and to this day only a causeway links the island to the Danish mainland, but it is also linked by ferry to the German island of Sylt.

Near the main building, and connected to it by a glazed walkway – a source of shelter in cold weather – is a separate swimming-pool house. There is also an outdoor tennis court not far away.

LEFT **The bench-style sofa that fits so perfectly into the space by the windows is a design by architects Schmidt Hammer Lassen, while the freestanding furniture is by Hans J. Wegner. On the shelf above the sofa rests a pair of binoculars for birdwatching, a favourite pastime of the owners. The rug is by the Finnish designer Ritva Puotila for Woodnotes.**

THE HOUSE IS FILLED WITH CHAIRS AND TABLES BY HANS J. WEGNER, A GREAT MASTER OF 20TH-CENTURY DANISH FURNITURE DESIGN, WHOSE WORK STRIKES A STRONG CHORD WITH JAPANESE FURNITURE-BUYERS.

THIS PAGE AND OPPOSITE **From the famous Wishbone (Y) chair of 1950 to the 1980s Hoop chair, the creations of Hans J. Wegner take pride of place in the light-filled rooms. They represent the pinnacle of Danish furniture design and work equally well in modern and more traditional settings. There are two fireplaces in the house.**

The main house consists of about 370 square metres of floor space, which is more than enough when only two people are living there. The owners use it at all times of the year, whenever they can take time off from their work in the fashion business.

Modern fire precautions mean that the construction of thatched roofs is subject to strict controls; repairing existing roofs is not generally a problem, but creating a new thatched roof requires meticulous adherence to building regulations. Happily, this particular roof has caused hardly any concern; the only work that needed to be done, some ten years after its construction, was to replace its exposed protective covering. The present owners dismiss the prospect of any future maintenance problems; they argue that, if this building method has worked satisfactorily for hundred of years, why should it not work now? When you consider the comparative fragility of more modern structures, it is easy to sympathize with their view.

So is this thatched structure a typical traditional Danish building or a thoroughly modern living space? It depends on whom you ask. Emphasizing its exposed internal load-bearing laminated-wood columns and windowsills, the architects see it as representing a building type that can be traced back to a technique used by the Vikings.

For modern viewers of this elegant home, the traditional houses of Japan, and Kyoto in particular, immediately spring to mind. As the present owners acknowledge, this association is underlined by the black prefabricated wooden elements with shutters that make up the façade. The house is filled with chairs and tables designed by Hans J. Wegner, one of the leading lights of 20th-century Danish furniture design. In recent years, Wegner's designs have struck a powerful chord with Japanese furniture-buyers, who see them as the perfect complement to paper walls, tatami mats and handcrafted Kiyomizu ceramics. The cultural connection between Japan and Scandinavia is strong, based on the principle that less is more.

The love of simplicity is also exemplified by the large fireplace that stands in the centre of the ground-floor living room. The fireplace is a smooth white cube from floor to ceiling, with a dark granite frame sunk into the wooden floor to prevent the floor from being marked by sparks from the fire. The colour of the fireplace is out of character

OPPOSITE **Despite the generous size of the house, every available space is put to good use, as in a well-designed yacht. In the kitchen, wine bottles are stored above the door and olive oil and vinegar are kept above the oven, within easy reach of the cook. Appliances are built into the walls. The structural details of the house have been allowed to remain visible, thereby forming a decorative element.**

LEFT **Every nook and cranny has been used to fit bookshelves and cupboards to maximize the space and keep clutter out of sight.**

RIGHT **The Japanese influence is most clearly seen in the walkway to the pool house, which is flanked by wooden screens.**

BELOW **The nautical inspiration is evident in the bunk beds installed in the guest room.**

with the functionality seen elsewhere; white is not the most practical surface colour for a fireplace, but it is still very common in Scandinavian houses, in particular in mid-20th-century buildings, but also in new houses such as this one.

The visible ceiling construction and the many built-in cupboards and shelves are reminiscent of the interior of a cleverly designed yacht. The wood that has been used to make the ceiling and the cupboards has been left without paint or stain so that its natural appearance is intact, with every knot and grain line visible. The cupboards and shelves are used to contain all the clutter of daily life, and thereby to keep the sight lines from the inside to the outside uninterrupted. The garden is an extension of the relaxed style of the interior; it is well maintained, but shrubs and bushes are allowed to grow free.

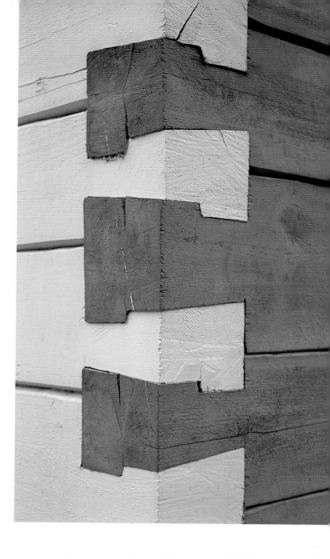

THIS PAGE AND OPPOSITE **Modern yet traditional, the Vistet house relies on ancient construction techniques. It looks as if it has been in its location for more than a hundred years, despite being transported around Sweden for three years until 2000. In a way, it is the ultimate Swedish country house, but it is also a document of the present. If Sweden sent a time capsule into space that included a house to show Martians how the Swedes live today, the Vistet house would be the building chosen. Yet, it is still a unique building that represents only itself and not the norm. The apparently randomly placed windows owe more to Le Corbusier than to ancient Swedish farmers, but the timber joints clearly have their origins in traditional Swedish house building. It is easy to see who contributed what to the design: the windows by Sandell, the construction by Landström. The present owner has discovered the right location for the house's ultimate resting place, yet it was not designed for any specific location. When the grass grows up around it, no one will be able to tell.**

MOVING **LODGE**

The Vistet house, also known as the Lodge, was designed by architects Thomas Sandell and Anders Landström in 1997. It was shown in Kalmar and Stockholm before it settled down with its current owner in the outer Stockholm archipelago.

The original purpose of the Vistet house was to demonstrate how 18th-century building techniques could be regarded as environmentally friendly and energy efficient at the end of the 20th century. It required two skilled architects and a team of equally skilled timber builders. Once completed, the house was put on show in 1997 in the Swedish city of Kalmar during the 600th jubilee of the 1397 Kalmar Union, a political agreement that united Scandinavia. The house was then moved to Stockholm in time for the 1998 European Capital of Culture celebrations. It was placed outside the entrance of Nordiska Museet (the Nordic Museum), the national Swedish museum for culture after 1520, and opened to the public from February to December 1998.

Finally, the Vistet house was put up for auction and bought by Nils Tunebjer and his family. Tunebjer did not have a plot of land to put the house on; indeed, he had had no intention of bidding at the auction. But when the bidding was slow, he was tempted, and ended up owning a unique house. What made the house even more interesting for him was that, while two well-known architects had designed it in a modern style, its timber construction followed old Swedish building technology, with interlocking beam-ends and internally visible trunks of timber.

The Vistet architect Thomas Sandell is – together with Gert Wingårdh and the trio Claesson Koivisto Rune – among the best-known Swedish architects of modern times. A former president of SAR, the National Association of Swedish Architects, he taught architecture to Victoria, the Crown Princess of Sweden. As a furniture designer, Sandell has collaborated with several Swedish and foreign furniture producers: Artek, Asplund, B&B Italia, Cappellini, CBI, Gärsnäs, IKEA, Källemo, Mobileffe and Tronconi. His interiors include the Stockholm stock exchange, the Wallpaper House in Milan in 1999, the restaurant at the Museum of Modern Art in Stockholm, the Ericsson office in London, and several noted Stockholm restaurants such as East and Rolfs Kök; the latter is now a listed interior.

Thomas Sandell's style has repeatedly been described as typically Swedish (even though he is originally from Finland), and he has often been

THIS PAGE AND OPPOSITE **Some of the most renowned Swedish designers collaborated on the original interior of the Vistet house when it was exhibited. Owner Nils Tunebjer has picked out the best of the best. The dining table is by Johan Edjemo for Asplund, with a pendant light above it by Katrin Hefter; the dining chairs are by John Kandell for Källemo. The dotted rug is by Pia Wallén for Asplund, while the interlocking stools, called wedding stools, are by Thomas Sandell for Asplund. Beside the fireplace is a Code firewood basket in white-lacquered steel by Ola Vihlborg for Asplund, while the cubes in front of it are by Katrin Hefter. The armchairs, called Box, are by Pierro Lissoni for Living Divani.**

held up as a flag carrier of the connection between the old and the new in Swedish design. This may be reading too much into his work, however; he is basically a modern designer.

The other Vistet architect, Anders Landström, specializes in timber construction, a skill gained during his childhood in northern Sweden, where it has been the norm since houses were first built hundreds of years ago. Apart from private homes, he is also responsible for the Swedish Embassy in Pretoria, South Africa, and the repair of many older buildings. With regard to Vistet, he points out how well a traditional timber construction keeps dry inside and how suitable it is for people with allergies since it incorporates nothing but natural materials. While concrete might be easier to shape, timber is a very economical material, both environmentally and in monetary terms. Even in Scandinavia, this is a fact worth repeating.

TRADITIONAL COUNTRY

OPPOSITE **The vertical bookshelf is a Swedish classic from 1989: the Pilaster by John Kandell for Källemo. The chaise longue is called Charles, by Antonio Citterio for B&B Italia. The pleated floor lamp is by Katrin Hefter for the now defunct Swedish furniture company CBI. The metal armchair is called the Thinking Man's Chair and was designed in 1988 for the Italian company Cappellini by Jasper Morrison. The interlocking wedding stools by Thomas Sandell were also used extensively in the Swedish ambassador's residence in Berlin, specially made in walnut to match the ambassador's grand piano, but here made in oiled oak. On the wall is a white plastic clock called Camp by Mårten Claesson, Eero Koivisto and Ola Rune for David Design.**

RIGHT **A mobile designed by Alexander Calder, from the Danish company Flensted, hangs from the ceiling of the guest house.**

After he had bought the Vistet house, the first problem for Nils Tunebjer was where to store it until he found somewhere to put it up. Luckily, the house came with its own carpenter, who had helped to build it and who now had the task of taking it apart piece by piece.

While trying to decide where to erect the house, Tunebjer thought of the outer south Stockholm archipelago, whose pebbled beaches, pine trees, cliffs and austere landscape would make a good setting for the building. He bought a plot of land on a remote island and had the house rebuilt. He also asked Anders Landström to design two smaller, matching guesthouses, placed at a 90-degree angle to the main house so that the plan resembled an old farmstead. The house was already fitted with a solid-wood kitchen designed by Sandell, with a worktop made from cast iron treated against rust. Landström designed a new fireplace. Electricity, plumbing and hot water were installed.

The Tunebjer family uses the house all year round, even during the tough Scandinavian winters. The island where the house stands is so far out into the Baltic that the open waters around it never freeze. Instead, ice flakes are pushed onto the island and stack up on the beach by the house, sometimes creating piles up to 3 metres tall. The winds and waves are strong around the island; it is one of the few places in Sweden where you can surf. But the thick timber construction keeps the house as warm inside as any modern insulation material, and the raw timber roof has not required any maintenance since it was built. It's a matter of quality through and through, says Tunebjer.

≪≪ **THE OUTER SOUTH STOCKHOLM ARCHIPELAGO, WITH ITS PEBBLED BEACHES, PINE TREES, CLIFFS AND AUSTERE LANDSCAPE, MADE A SUITABLE SETTING FOR THE RECONSTRUCTED BUILDING.** ≫≫

ELEMENTAL COUNTRY

Wherever you are in Scandinavia, even in the big cities, nature is never very far distant. Fulfilling the dream of living close to nature does not require sophisticated buildings; on the contrary, some of the best homes are the simplest ones. It is the awareness of the natural elements of air, water, earth and fire – and how these elements are incorporated in the design and construction of the houses – that makes all the difference.

LEFT The 200-year-old timber creates a dark but restful interior. The only light sources except the small windows are oil lamps, candles and the fireplace, but then the Finnish summer nights are never dark. The winter is a different matter, but then the house is usually not lived in.

RIGHT Mass-produced designs are few in the Puotila household, but on the floor is a Pirkka stool designed by Ilmari Tapiovaara in 1955, now again in production by the Finnish company Aero. The stool is one of the originals.

Ritva Puotila and her husband built their first house on Lake Saimaa in 1965. Today there are seven buildings on their property, including the original main house, a kitchen house, a wood-fired sauna and additional sleeping cabins for guests. In common with many Finnish country houses, these are without electricity and running water. Fresh water has to be brought from the mainland, a short boat journey away. The whole estate covers slightly less than a hectare, and the only other inhabitants of the island are Puotila relatives.

There is nothing modern or attention-seeking about the houses. Ritva Puotila hails from Vyborg, nowadays part of Russia. Her roots are deep in the Carelian culture, as is the ascetic approach to life. The logs used to build the houses are dead wood from Lapland in northern Finland, greyed over time by snow and cold. The windows – where there are any to be found – are small and the furniture is old, some from the early 19th century. There are textiles in abundance in the houses, including old Carelian textiles collected over many years. There are also old kitchen utensils and baskets, inherited from previous generations and put to new uses.

Ritva Puotila herself is the *grande dame* of Finnish textile design, having worked actively in the business for more than 50 years. Her interest in textiles began when she was a child, and in the 1950s she started to participate in design competitions, winning several prizes and grants in Finnish rya rug design competitions. She also won first prize in a design competition for fashion textiles, arranged by Villayhtymä, the largest wool factory in Finland at the time.

Soon after graduating, Ritva Puotila received her first international award, a gold medal at the XII Milan Triennial, again for a rya rug. In 1961 she was awarded first prize for designing

CARELIA **DREAMING**

Saimaa, Finland's largest lake, has over 13,000 islands. The Puotila houses are on one of those islands, in the district of Carelia, less than 30 km from the Russian border. While the houses look centuries old, they were actually built from 1965.

OPPOSITE, BOTTOM LEFT **The Sámi boots used to belong to Puotila's sons, all long since grown up. The upturned fronts are typical of the traditional Sámi boots that are still in use in Lapland.**

OPPOSITE, OTHER PICTURES **Birch and pine are the two dominant trees in Finland, usually growing happily together. While the pine recalls the famous Finnish melancholy and the dark winters, the birch is a symbol of summer and happiness. The ground is usually covered with moss and bushes, and rocks in the open.**

ABOVE **The cabin is free for guests who wants to leave a dinner in the kitchen house early to enjoy some soothing sleep. A long day out on a boat or walking in the woods, followed by sauna and dinner, is enough to make anyone tired.**

RIGHT, SMALL PICTURES **The main house is adorned by a long balcony overlooking Lake Saimaa. Part of the balustrade in front of the house has been made into a bench, long enough to take half a dozen people, but it is equally pleasant simply to sit alone there and read.**

RIGHT **In summer the nights never get dark, so the spectacular view over the lake can be appreciated to the full. Most meals are taken out in the open, unless a warm summer rain starts to fall. Usually, the only other disturbance is created by mosquitoes, which are famously fierce and annoying in this region.**

On account of its curving shoreline, Lake Saimaa has the second longest shoreline of any lake in the world, although it is not the second largest lake.

The wood-fired sauna house, built in 1991, has the thickest timbers of all the houses on the Puotila estate. There are three basic sauna types in Finland: electric, wood-fired with chimney, and wood-fired without chimney. The last is the oldest and most traditional type, and the one Puotila

LEFT AND BELOW **The kitchen house is dark with soot from the fireplace, which, like everything else, was built by hand, piece by piece. The long bench is made entirely of wood with no nails or screws holding it together. Note the large crossbeam in the ceiling.**

OPPOSITE **The dining table is one of the oldest objects in the houses, some 200 years old. Its intricate construction means that it could easily pass as an artwork. The chairs appear distinctly Finnish but they are actually by a contemporary but traditional French company, made in chestnut. There is a rya rug on the wall behind.**

THERE IS NOTHING MODERN OR ATTENTION-SEEKING ABOUT THE HOUSES. LIKE MANY FINNISH COUNTRY HOMES, THEY HAVE NO ELECTRICITY OR RUNNING WATER. FRESH WATER HAS TO BE BROUGHT FROM THE MAINLAND, A SHORT BOAT JOURNEY AWAY.

table textiles for the American company Dansk. These prizes enabled Puotila to establish her own studio and to start a career as freelance designer for several companies in Scandinavia, the USA and the Far East. The American work led to cooperation with the Finnish company Tampella, owner of the biggest linen mill in Scandinavia at that time. In addition to interior textiles, Tampella manufactured engineering products and used paper yarn for insulating cables. Puotila was able to make use of the very specialist knowledge that she had acquired while working for Tampella when she set up the company Woodnotes in the late 1980s, working with spun paper fibres.

The waters of Lake Saimaa are just in front of the houses. The lake is relatively shallow, so it heats up easily in summer. Some 7,000 years ago, Saimaa was part of the Baltic Sea, and when it became cut off at the end of the last ice age, a population of seals was trapped. These have developed into a distinct species, known as Saimaa seals.

THIS PAGE AND OPPOSITE **The sauna is a separate building. Fire is always a potential danger in traditional wood-fired saunas, but it is not just a matter of fire safety. Finnish country houses seldom have electricity, and the wood-fired saunas are much preferred anyway. The heat is less dry than in electric saunas, and the whole experience is felt to be much more authentic. Outside in a bucket are birch twigs with which to slap the back in the heat, together with a scoop to use to throw water on the sauna's hot stones. A Woodnotes rug, designed by Puotila, adorns the decking.**

THE WOOD-FIRED SAUNA HAS THE THICKEST TIMBERS OF ALL THE HOUSES ON THE PUOTILA ESTATE. THIS IS FINLAND'S OLDEST AND MOST TRADITIONAL TYPE OF SAUNA.

has. Once the fire has died down, the sauna can be entered. Throwing water on the still-hot stones surrounding the fire will make the room fill with steam. After 10 to 20 minutes in the hot, humid air, it is time to jump into the lake and then back to the sauna again.

Ritva Puotila has been the subject of numerous solo exhibitions, including appearances in some 20 cities in the USA, as well as in Japan, Denmark, Sweden, Norway, Iceland and Finland. Since 1959 she has also participated in joint exhibitions all over the world. Her textile artworks feature in the collections of many European museums of applied arts, in the collections of the American Craft Museum, and in the Design and Architecture Collection of the Museum of Modern Art in New York. Her unique textile art adorns both the headquarters of the Bank of Finland in Helsinki and the Council of the European Union building in Brussels.

In Finland, Ritva Puotila has received numerous accolades for her work, including the Finland Prize, the Kaj Franck Design Prize, Textile Artist of the Year, and the prestigious Pro Finlandia medal in 2003, presented by the president. In 2004, Puotila was conferred

with an honorary doctorate at the University of Lapland for her work as a textile artist and designer. After so many years of designing contemporary textiles and all the attention lavished upon her, she still returns each summer to the rustic houses on the island in Lake Saimaa. This is where she can gather her energy before returning to city life.

THIS PAGE **Now you see it . . . now you don't. Finnish county homes are never designed to make a big splash in their location; instead, the priority is that they should blend in with the surroundings.**

OPPOSITE, TOP **While the Swedish part of the archipelago between Finland and Sweden is green and lush, the Finnish side is austere, with naked rocks and crumbling pine trees – features reflected in the Finnish style of architecture.**

ROCKY **RETREAT**

This house is perhaps the proudest but most modest of all those featured in this book. It is simply a functional rural home, made to be in harmony with nature and to shelter its owner. Built in 1967, it reflects the skill of a generation of Finnish country-house builders.

ABOVE **The Baltic Sea is calm in summer, and warm enough for swimming, but in winter the ice is thick enough to support a car. Environmental pollution from the former Soviet states surrounding the Baltic makes the water far from pure, and the Swedish and Finnish governments have invested heavily in helping the new states with water-cleaning technology.**

Mikko Pulkkinen, an architect by profession, built his country house on a small island, near the larger island of Kustavi, in 1967. The islands are part of the Turku archipelago, named after the old capital of Finland, and lie close to the Finnish mainland. The house is only 52 square metres in area, with Pulkkinen and his family owning some 5 hectares of the island; close relatives own the other 5 hectares.

The house was entirely planned and built by Pulkkinen, who chose the location very carefully. While he wanted a full view of the sea, he did not want to have to endure the full force of the sea wind. Therefore, the house was placed in a sunken area just above a large cliff, which channels the wind up and over the cliff, and provides protection for the house while the sea remains visible. From the water, all that can be seen are the

two tall red chimneys protruding above the granite face of the cliff. Large rocks and boulders that look as if they have been deliberately placed there by the owner for aesthetic reasons surround the house. In fact, these are relics of the last ice age, when great boulders were dragged through Scandinavia as the ice expanded and contracted, and left randomly scattered when the ice melted. Alder, rowan and pine, trees that are abundant in the area, also flank the house.

The exterior of the house is clad in birchwood stained dark grey. The original windows were replaced some years ago; the old single glazing was good only for summer visits, but the new windows allow Pulkkinen and his family to stay at the house in winter as well.

Like most Finns, Pulkkinen takes an unbroken five-week holiday each year, starting in late June. Another week is usually saved for winter, often timed to coincide with the schools' winter sports break, an important holiday for a nation whose national sports are ice hockey and cross-country skiing. Even in families whose children have long

since left school, the winter holiday week remains a tradition. Pulkkinen also spends most weekends of the year at his country house.

Unless it is an unusually warm year, the first blocks of ice start to form on the sea in October, making travel by boat difficult. By January, the ice is strong enough to walk on and to support the traditional kick sledge, still popular in Finland as a way of getting about in a snow-covered landscape. The ice usually lingers until April, with the last traces sometimes even staying until May.

The fact that the island is a virtual delicatessen is a great attraction, since, for many Finns, the food is a highlight of their country visits. The sea supplies fresh fish in abundance, while the forests are rich in wild berries and mushrooms. The fish is

OPPOSITE AND ABOVE **The dining area is at one with the outside. Seabirds abound on the island, but instead of shooting them, Pulkkinen has simply displayed above the window what the birds have chosen to leave behind.**

ABOVE RIGHT **The enamelled coffee pot on the stove was designed by Antti Nurmesniemi for Arabia Wärtsilä in 1955. This design classic is seen in many Finnish homes.**

« THE SEA SUPPLIES FRESH FISH IN ABUNDANCE, WHILE THE FORESTS ARE RICH IN BERRIES AND MUSHROOMS . . . THE LARGE TRAY ON THE KITCHEN WALL, BOUGHT IN SINGAPORE, IS USED TO DRY MUSHROOMS. »

usually cooked on an outdoor grill or barbecue, while the mushrooms and berries are eaten fresh or used in stews and pies. There is also a strong tradition in Finland of enjoying high-quality sausages, a legacy of the time when the merchants of the German Hansa were influential in the region, and these are also delicious cooked on the grill. Finland has some excellent lagers, of which Lapin Kulta (the Gold of Lapland) and Karhu (the Bear) are the most popular. These are drunk cold as an accompaniment to whatever nature has provided for the meal. Not far

from the house is also a small greenhouse, which supplies spinach, salad and tomatoes in summer.

Efficient use of space is vital in a small house. The beds, which incorporate storage for bedlinen, were constructed by a local carpenter according to Pulkkinen's plans. The main fireplace has a two-tier metal construction that allows logs to be kept underneath. The coffee and dining tables are

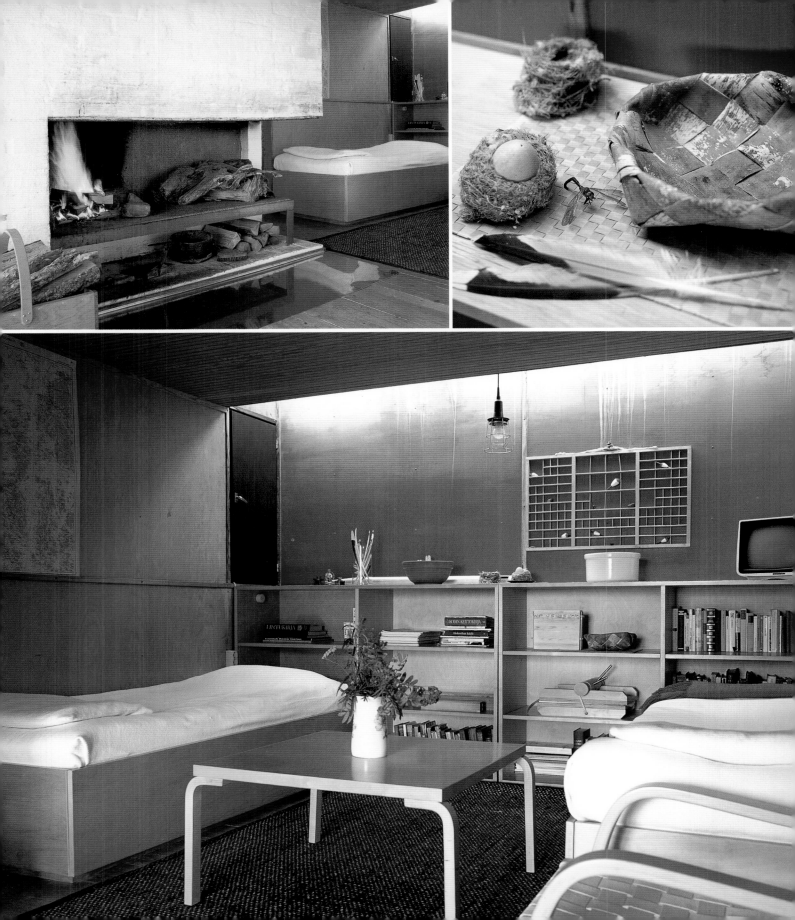

supported by the famous L-shaped legs by Alvar Aalto for his company Artek – a 1930s design – but Pulkkinen has made his own tabletops. The ceiling lights are adapted from lamps commonly used on building sites. To make the most of natural illumination, a large ceiling window has been installed to admit shafts of sunlight into the house. The beds have been placed close to the fireplace to obtain maximum warmth on cold nights. The custom-made shelves contain reminders of the natural world: eagle feathers, a dragonfly and eider duck nests containing abandoned eggs.

By the kitchen window is a stack of unusual matchboxes in a holder on the wall. They were specially made for Mikko Pulkkinen's son's wedding, showing a picture of the bride and groom standing on a cliff not dissimilar to the cliffs on the island. Today they are used for lighting the gas-fired stove to prepare the next meal.

ABOVE AND ABOVE LEFT **Armchair 406 was designed by Alvar Aalto for Artek in 1938–39; the bentwood construction means that it adapts to the position of the body. The classic version is in pale birch with natural linen straps, as here. The curtain design is by Vuokko Nurmesniemi, famous for her work for the Finnish textile company Marimekko.**

BELOW **The birchwood used in the house's façade is stained dark grey.**

OPPOSITE, ABOVE LEFT **The nights can be very cold on the islands, so the beds are placed near the fire.**

OPPOSITE, ABOVE RIGHT **Woven baskets like this one can still be found at Finnish farmers' fairs, held on Saturdays and Sundays, even in Helsinki. It is made by a traditional craft that involves drying and weaving strips of the soft inner bark from a birch tree. The basket is used for picking wild berries.**

OPPOSITE, BELOW **The coffee-table legs are by Alvar Aalto for Artek, a suitable design contribution to the nation with the world's highest coffee consumption. The old black-and-white television set is by Finlux – a company that reigned supreme in Finland before Sony came along.**

The west coast of Sweden has a landscape quite distinct from the greener Stockholm archipelago on the eastern side of Sweden, which is set in the Baltic Sea. The west coast faces straight onto the Atlantic and has a very different environment from that in the east, with different species of wildlife both above and below the water line.

People from the west coast of Sweden are quick to point out that they live at 'the front of Sweden' while the capital, Stockholm, is situated at 'the back'. There is a certain truth in this; the people of the west coast have relied for many generations on seafaring and shipping, and it is much closer not only to Norway and Denmark but also to Britain and the continent. Sweden's second largest city is Gothenburg, the capital of the west coast, sometimes referred to as Little London on account of its proximity to the British capital across the water. Besides shipping, the car manufacturer Volvo has its base at Gothenburg and has brought wealth to the region for many years.

Halland is the region starting just south of Gothenburg, stretching south along the coast until it reaches Skåne, like Halland itself a part of old Denmark. The main cities in Halland are Halmstad and Varberg, neither of them particularly large but both very popular in summer. Halland is Sweden's prime golf region. Mild winters and early springs contribute to a long playing season, and within Halland's borders there are some 30 golf courses.

It is no surprise, then, that the owner of this house in south-western Sweden is proud to be the possessor of some 53 hectares of woodland, fields and islands along the popular coast of Halland. The estate includes an old farmstead and a 1930s stone house, but the architect Peter Hulting was called in to design three new buildings: the cabin, its matching outhouse, and the main house, to be completed in 2007. At the moment, the cabin is used by the owners, but it will be turned into a guesthouse once the main building is completed. The Atlantic Ocean is nearby, reaching up to the property through a shallow bay.

The cabin is very straightforward in its layout, consisting in essence of one long room with a high-pitched ceiling. The room combines all the functions; it is kitchen, dining room, sleeping area

THIS PAGE AND OPPOSITE **The dining chairs are CH29 by Hans J. Wegner from 1952, manufactured by Carl Hansen & Sons of Denmark. The pendant lamp is the classic PH5 by Poul Henningsen from 1958 for Louis Poulsen, reputedly hanging in half of all Danish homes. The sofa below the window is by the Swede Bruno Mathsson.**

CABIN **FEVER**

Peter Hulting designed this cabin in south-western Sweden for a client who owns a large estate. While the cabin looks comfortable enough, it is awaiting its big brother. The cabin is only a guesthouse, which will have a much larger main house built next to it.

and living room all in one. Only the shower and WC are behind doors. The entire floor is covered in concrete that has deliberately been left unpolished. It still retains some of the roughness from when it was first put down, but has been clear-lacquered to stop it from giving off dust. The main material of the walls and ceiling is spruce, but the spruce has been mixed up with fir for a more uneven appearance.

The large window frames for the sliding doors are in lacquered steel, while the outside shutters are in Siberian larch. Hulting decided to put the sliding shutters outside rather than inside the windows for two reasons. First, it means that the windows can be open in summer while the shutters shield the interior from the heat, and second, the outside shutters make the cabin look more like an industrial shed than a pretty little country house. The exterior of the cabin has been stained silver-grey to reinforce the utilitarian look. The roof tiles are old and recycled, originally made in the 1920s.

The dining chairs and easy chair are by Hans J. Wegner, while the pendant over the dining table is an old PH5 by Poul Henningsen. The dining table is from IKEA and so are the stainless-steel fronts of the

ABOVE LEFT AND ABOVE **The easy chair, like the dining chairs, is by Hans J. Wegner. The fireplace and the floor are made of concrete. Behind the hanging textile are a wardrobe and a sleeping area.**

RIGHT **The structural frame around the cooking area is made from painted MDF. The kitchen is 90 cm deep; it was deliberately made the same depth as the shower room and WC to the right of it so that the wall would be one unbroken line. The thick stainless-steel worktop was specially made for the cabin and chosen by the architect. The dining table is from IKEA, as are the kitchen cupboards with stainless-steel fronts. The colourful kitchen tiles are from Portugal.**

THIS PICTURE The Atlantic Ocean, in the form of a shallow bay, is just beyond the cliffs visible from the bedroom area. The deep window frames also serve as bookshelves; the edges were made to stick out into the room to give more surface.

≪≪ THE CABIN CONSISTS SIMPLY OF ONE SPACE THAT COMBINES LIVING AREA, DINING ROOM, KITCHEN AND SLEEPING AREA. ≫≫

kitchen cupboards. The brightly coloured tiles behind the kitchen work surface are from Portugal. The sofa is by the Swedish architect and designer Bruno Mathsson. The chair in the bedroom is an old painted birch chair that has been stripped of its paint.

The structural stability of the house was put to a severe test by Gudrun, a storm with hurricane-force winds that hit Scandinavia on the weekend of 8–9 January 2005, while the owners were staying there. Across Scandinavia, 17 people were killed during the storm and another ten during the clearing up. In Sweden, five nuclear reactors were shut down and all railway traffic was suspended. In southern Sweden, 400,000 homes were deprived of electricity, and in the worst-hit areas neither mobiles nor fixed telephones worked.

Gudrun felled 75 million cubic metres of forest in Sweden alone, almost equalling the country's annual felling total. The little cabin in Halland escaped relatively lightly, but the wind moved it by a small fraction, and the concrete floor cracked in places. The damage is still visible but will soon be repaired. It took weeks before the cabin had its electricity supply restored, and the storm gave the owners a memory they will never forget.

ABOVE **The outhouse with its wall-mounted bench is visible through the bedroom window. It has been made exactly the same size as the cabin: 50 square metres.**

RIGHT **To underline the utilitarian look created by the large shutters, the wooden façade of the cabin has been stained silver-grey. The roof tiles are old and recycled, originally made in the 1920s. The outhouse is used for tools.**

THIS PICTURE The sofa and coffee table were both specially made for the house, while the easy chairs in front are from IKEA. The furniture, like the floor, is made from aspen; walls and ceilings are ash.

RIGHT The low bench along the front of the fireplace is made of concrete. The large artwork above the mantel is by the Norwegian artist Geis Harald Samuelsen and is made from sheets of lead sprayed with high-gloss automotive paint.

MODERN **NATURAL**

With a nature reserve as neighbour and wild sheep grazing around the corner, this could have been another romantic Norwegian cottage. Instead, it is a sparsely furnished box where concrete is king. When the 50 best Norwegian buildings of the past five years were chosen, this was the only new country house included.

The house is located on an island in Vestfold, on the western side of the Oslo fjord. The nearest larger town is Tønsberg. This is an area that has been colonized by summer visitors from Oslo since the early 20th century, and the population now increases by almost tenfold during the holiday season. The district has a rich wildlife, including many species of seabird, elk, deer and even lynx. Mink can sometimes be seen on the smaller islands furthest out to sea. The southern point of Tjøme island is known as Verdens Ende – the World's End – and overlooks the open sea.

The house was built in 2003 and designed by the architects Lund Hagem, a relatively large firm headed by Suein Lund and Einar Hagem, among whose many projects is a country house for the King of Norway. Designed to provide shelter from the wind, this

house opens up towards a courtyard at the centre. The idea was to use as few materials and colours as possible to give the house a calm and unified appearance. The three main materials are concrete, aspen and ash wood, with a colour palette of greys and natural wood.

The area between the house and the open sea is a nature reserve, which the public are free to visit but not to build on. In Norway, as in many other countries, building is prohibited along the coast in order to protect it for future generations. But the seafront can be enjoyed in many other ways. The family who live in this house keep both a small motorboat for fishing and two kayaks that they use frequently to explore the neighbouring islands and skerries.

Most of the furniture in the house has been specially made for this location and fixed to the wall to create the impression that it is part of the

ABOVE **Kitchen units are custom-made, like all other fixed furniture in the house, while the kitchen appliances are from Miele. Instead of large overhanging cabinets, a free-hanging shelf was installed so that the kitchen area would retain its light appearance.**

RIGHT **The dining table, sofa and bookshelves are all built in ash and made specially for the house. Simple teak chairs like those used in the courtyard are also used for dining. The small pendant lights are from the Danish company Herstal. A slanted skylight illuminates the dining area and kitchen.**

OPPOSITE AND RIGHT **The kitchen worktop is made of concrete, like many other parts of the house. Most of the glass items above it are by Benny Motzfeldt (1909–95), who was a pioneer in Norwegian glass design. She worked for Christiania Glassmagasin, Hadeland and Randsfjord glassworks and the Plus glass studio in Fredrikstad.**

BELOW **The wooden floor in the bathroom is laid with gaps between the floorboards so that water can run between them. Underneath is a concrete screed with a hole for the water to run out, and underfloor heating. The floor planks are loose so that they can easily be removed for cleaning underneath.**

« THE IDEA WAS TO USE AS FEW MATERIALS AND COLOURS AS POSSIBLE TO GIVE THE HOUSE A CALM AND UNIFIED APPEARANCE. THE THREE PRINCIPAL MATERIALS ARE CONCRETE, ASPEN AND ASH, WITH A COLOUR PALETTE OF GREYS AND NATURAL WOOD. »

structure and to keep loose items to a minimum. The ash used for the bespoke furniture matches the ash of the floor to bring the two together. The ash bookshelves are integrated with the walls rather than freestanding. It requires a certain discipline to keep the house free of clutter, but the owners have succeeded well in this.

The house in Vestfold is used mainly in summer. Norwegians are very enthusiastic about outdoor sports and exercise, perhaps even more so than their Scandinavian neighbours. Skiing is a popular sport for the house owners and in winter they usually stay in a cabin in the mountains further north, close to the ski slopes. But they like to visit their coastal country home around Christmas.

Natural vegetation has been allowed to encroach on the building without much interference. A small area near the house has been covered with sand for ball games, and there are wild rose bushes and juniper bushes growing nearby. The courtyard has a vine-covered wall that produces grapes each summer.

The concrete-covered courtyard is framed by a sunken strip filled with round stones of various sizes that have been collected from the area by the owners. This is an endless project since each walk along the beach or meadow might bring up another decorative stone, shaped by nature over the years. The dining table in the courtyard is also made from concrete, while the outdoor dining chairs are of the same type as used around the indoor dining table. The courtyard has a shower with a large head that is used in summer.

ABOVE LEFT **The courtyard is designed to be protected from the wind. One wall is covered with a grapevine that gives fruit each summer. Natural vegetation has been allowed to encroach on the house, and there are wild roses and juniper bushes flourishing nearby.**

LEFT **Concrete is the material used to make the dining table in the courtyard. The outdoor chairs are of the same type as those used for dining indoors. The courtyard shower is used in summer; when the weather is clement, it is preferred to its counterpart indoors.**

BELOW AND BELOW LEFT **The concrete is framed by a sunken strip filled with round stones collected from the area by the owners, each chosen for its special appeal.**

The wooden flooring in the bathroom has been laid with gaps between the boards so that splashed water is able to run between them. Underneath is a concrete screed with a hole for the water to run out, and underfloor heating; the floor planks are loose so that they can easily be removed for cleaning underneath. This creates a perfectly functional floor while allowing the wood used in the rest of the house to appear in the bathroom. The concrete frame that the bathtub sits in continues out through the window by the end of the tub to become an outdoor bench, so that there is a sense of indoor and outdoor coming together while you are in the bath.

The National Museum in Oslo recently mounted an exhibition of the ten best buildings constructed in Norway each year over the past five years, making 50 buildings in total. Corporate, public and private buildings were included in the exhibition, but only two country houses. One was an addition to an existing structure, and the other was completely newly built. The second was the house in Vestfold, which proves that less can certainly be more.

ABOVE **Natural vegetation, including wild roses and juniper bushes, has been allowed to encroach on the building, and there is a nature reserve nearby.**

BELOW **Wild sheep can be seen grazing on the island throughout the year. The district's wildlife includes elk, deer and lynx as well as seabirds; mink can sometimes be seen on the smaller islands furthest out to sea.**

MID-CENTURY MODERN
COUNTRY

The mid-20th century saw a peak in Scandinavian design, but it was also a period of postwar economic hardship. Many city homes of the time have altered, but country houses are more likely to have been left unchanged. There is great interest today in mid-20th-century design, which makes items from the period collectable, and they fit well into modern interiors.

The country house of Elina Helenius and her partner Mika Mahlberg stands right on the beach of the largest lake in southern Finland, Lake Lohja. It was designed by the acclaimed Finnish architect Matti Sanaksenaho and completed in 2002. The house is built over one floor and occupies a total area of about 65 square metres.

The plot on which the house was built is next door to land owned by Elina Helenius's parents. It is quite common in Finland to divide up land so that space is made available to build a country house for the younger generation. In many cases, the land will have been acquired many years earlier, when prices were more affordable, and having your children as neighbours means that you are familiar with the character of the rural community.

It makes perfect sense if two generations living next door to each other share a sauna house between them, as is the case here. Finland, a nation of five million people, has some 1.5 million saunas. Both men and women bathe in the sauna, but never together except within the family. When friends are invited for a sauna, it is customary to

ABOVE **The exterior of the house is made of vertical pine planks stained brown-black. The pillars supporting the patio roof are fashioned from tree trunks sourced from nearby woodland, while the irregularly shaped window frames are filled with toughened glass. Steps lead through the garden down to the shore of Lake Lohja.**

agree who goes first, men or women. Often the women are invited to go first, out of courtesy, or if they will be preparing a dinner afterwards.

Finland has the highest proportion of second-home ownership in Europe – some 25 per cent of Finns own a second home – but it is not a symbol of wealth as in other countries. Owning a second home has more to do with a strong culture of spending time in the countryside and the fact that large parts of Finland are thinly populated so it is

ABOVE **The low bench by the front door was designed and built by Mika Mahlberg. The graphite grey seat is made from Indian cotton, while the cushion cover is a design by Elina Helenius. The ceramic lamp foot is an old design from the Arabia ceramics factory in Helsinki that has acquired a new shade. The wool rug is a gift from Helenius's mother.**

RIGHT AND TOP RIGHT **The door is finished in clear lacquer to contrast it with the brown-black façade. The door handle is made from a tree branch and provides a good grip.**

CENTRE RIGHT **Fishing is among the favourite holiday pastimes at Lake Lohja, and pike-perch is among the most important catches.**

UNDERSTATED **COMFORT**

Only one hour's drive from Helsinki, this house overlooks Lake Lohja, the largest lake in southern Finland. It was designed by the Finnish architect Matti Sanaksenaho. The house is owned by the textile and graphic designer Elina Helenius and her family; Helenius created the interior herself.

<< THE FLOOR IS CLEAR-LAQUERED PINE, WHILE THE WALLS ARE MADE FROM CONIFER VENEER; THIS ALLOWS THE GRAIN LINES AND COLOURS OF THE PALE WOODEN FLOOR TO REMAIN VISIBLE AND IS HIGHLY DECORATIVE. >>

ABOVE AND ABOVE LEFT **James Irvine designed these chairs for IKEA's PS collection. Sheepskins once used to warm the children's snow sledges have found a new use indoors. The cushion covers are Helenius's own design.**

OPPOSITE **The fireplace and staircase are made of slate from a quarry in Orivesi, southern Finland. The floor lamp is a prototype designed by Petri Vainio for Doctor Design, a Helsinki-based company for which Helenius also works.**

still affordable to buy land or country homes. But with many people moving to the Helsinki region, prices around the capital city are increasing. The archipelago and coast are also very popular.

The Helenius family use their country home all year round, but their single longest stay, often six weeks long, is in the summer. Like most Finns, they deliberately live a simple but comfortable life while there, without television and close to nature. The main food tends to be the dark Finnish rye bread and fresh fish from Lake Lohja.

In summer the windows are left free of curtains to admit maximum light. Doors are left wide open, so that nature is only a step away. Finland is one of the safest and least crime-ridden countries in the world, so locking the door is the exception rather than the rule in country homes. Textiles are more evident in winter, when a warmer feeling is required; curtains are hung and throws are put out.

Elina Helenius designed the interior of the house herself, a task for which she is more than well qualified. She started her design career at the Finnish textile company Marimekko in 1989 and stayed there until 1992. She had previously been a teacher of print design at Lahti Polytechnic and has been a lecturer at the University of Art and Design in Helsinki since 2003. She has also worked as a textile designer for the Finnish company Doctor Design since 2002. Many of her textile designs are used in the house.

Matti Sanaksenaho, the house's architect, studied at the Helsinki University of Technology and received his degree in architecture in 1993.

LEFT The kitchen chairs, by Ilmari Tapiovaara for Asko, are second-hand finds. The table is by IKEA, while the birch bowl is designed by Petri Vainio for Showroom Finland. The stripy textile runner is by Elina Helenius, also for Showroom Finland.

RIGHT Old and new Arabia crockery shares shelves above the worktop with two bowls by Lovisa Wattman for Höganäs Keramik, Sweden. The blue cups are from the hand-painted 1960s series Valencia by Ulla Procopé for Arabia, discontinued in 2002.

BELOW To make the best use of space, there is a Japanese-style raised sleeping alcove with storage for bed linen underneath; the sliding doors made from wood veneer. Inside are several cushions with covers designed by Helenius.

He founded his own office in 1991. He has taught architecture at the University of Technology and been a guest professor at Aarhus Arkitektskole in Denmark. One of his recent and most publicized projects was the St Henry's Ecumenical Art Chapel in Turku, built in 2005. It is a fantastic wooden church building that resembles an upturned boat.

The floor of the house is clear-lacquered pine, while the walls are made from conifer veneer; this allows the grain lines and colours of the pale wood to remain visible and is highly decorative. It is typical of Sanaksenaho's architecture – natural wood is a theme that he keeps returning to, and it is also very Finnish; Finland is the foremost timber nation in Scandinavia. The only contrasting material is the dark Finnish slate that has been used for the fireplace and spills over onto the floor and staircase around it. The light grout is a stark contrast to the dark stone and emphasizes the irregular pieces of slate.

To utilize space to the maximum, there is a raised sleeping alcove with storage underneath, and sliding doors to close it all off from the rest of the house. There is an obvious Japanese influence in the design. The kitchen is deliberately kept very basic, as befits a Finnish country house. It has open shelves above the worktop holding glass and crockery, mainly old and new Arabia ceramics. Instead of a splashback, Sanaksenaho has placed two long, narrow windows above the worktop that give wonderful views of the natural world.

LEFT AND RIGHT **The comfortable living area in the Mill House has a fireplace surrounded on all four sides by toughened glass, with a frame and hood of black lacquered steel. To create maximum air circulation for the fireplace, an electric fan has been installed in the chimney. The sofa, fabrics and coffee table on wheels were all specially made for the house. The floor is in grey limestone from the Swedish island of Öland. The desk lights above the sofa are the Archimoon K lamps by Philippe Starck for Flos. There is a sliding door leading to the garden.**

HOMAGE TO **THE SAUNA**

The Mill House, as this building is called, is distinctly Japanese, resembling a Zen master's teahouse. It is also very Swedish, designed by Karin Wingårdh and Gert Wingårdh, who together run Wingårdh Arkitektkontor, the most acclaimed and successful architects' office in Sweden, with about 110 employees.

The Mill House is located not far from Malmö, the third largest city in Sweden, in the flat farming land that makes up much of the south of the country. It is an annexe to a larger building, an old farmhouse converted into a country retreat for a family living in Malmö. There is also a former sheep-cote and a barn on the estate. The whole purpose of the building is to celebrate one of the most uniquely Scandinavian traditions, that of the sauna. The traditional rite of the sauna bath includes a dip in cold, natural waters, but the creek nearby was not sufficient. Instead, the architects have created a pool in front of the building.

It is not a large building, but that was never the architectural brief nor the point. Its total footprint is only 7 metres square. Still, it has enough room for guests to the main house to stay for the night, and it also has space for undressing, relaxing and enjoying the sauna experience. While the main building was designed by the wife of the family in collaboration with a different firm of architects, the Mill House was very much the husband's project, intended as a place where he could entertain friends and colleagues.

There was once an old mill house on this site, which was the same size as the present house, but it was in such a bad state that it was not worth renovating. The brief given for the house was restricted, but the Wingårdhs have worked on previous, larger projects with the same client. The small private house is an

LEFT AND BELOW LEFT **The kitchen ceiling is supported by enormous oak beams. It was hard to find beams of this size, which come from ancient trees; they are usually used only for the building of traditional ships. The unusual circular window adds an extra dimension to the room.**

OPPOSITE, SMALL PICTURES **The crisscross pattern on the window takes up the theme of the nearby sheep-cote, which has a similar crisscross-beamed façade, a traditional architectural feature in southern Sweden and Denmark. The projecting screens are made from corded willow. The garden furniture is in oak and the tabletop is grey limestone from the island of Öland. Replacing an old house with a new one brought an already mature garden.**

OPPOSITE, RIGHT **The nearby creek was not considered to be adequate for the bathing that traditionally takes place after a sauna. To make up for this, the architects created a pool in front of the building.**

unusual project for them; they only do about one a year. Their best-known building is probably the black and white flight-control tower at Arlanda airport in Stockholm, seen by anyone who passes through the airport. Embassies feature high on their list of regular work. A recent project was the highly acclaimed House of Sweden in Washington, DC, which includes the chancellery for the Swedish embassy, apartments, exhibition space and a conference centre. The Swedish embassy in Berlin, completed in 1999, has also been highly praised.

Oak and grey limestone from the island of Öland were the two main materials used to build the house. On the outside of the building, the oak panels have been burned with a torch to make them black and more water-resistant. The roof is made from untreated wood shavings, also in oak, a traditional building method in this part of Sweden that is commonly seen in old churches. In due course, the roof will be impregnated with tar. Even the gutters are made of oak; they are lined with zinc to protect them against the effects of water.

Inside, the ceiling is held up by huge exposed oak beams. It was a substantial challenge for the architects to locate oak beams of this size.

THIS PICTURE AND INSET **To complement the triangular window, a sailmaker was called in to make curtains that open and close using the same mechanism as that used to raise and lower a sail. The floor lamp is from the Akari series of 1951 by Isamu Noguchi, handmade in Gifu, Japan, from washi paper and bamboo ribbing, and supported by a metal frame.**

RIGHT, ABOVE AND BELOW **The chair is the classic Lamino by Yngve Ekström from 1955, made by Swedese. The bed is made from oak, just like the building itself.**

OPPOSITE **The curving bench is made from abachi wood, a hard version of balsa wood, which is ideal for saunas since it does not absorb heat. Traditional park benches inspired the shape. The traditional-looking sauna heater is Finnish; the Finns are the masters of sauna equipment.**

ABOVE AND ABOVE RIGHT **The shower cubicle is made from limestone cut in triangular shapes to make the curve smoother; rectangular stones would have made the joints spikier. The sauna door pivots on only one point.**

The trees from which they came must have been growing for centuries to attain such a girth and are usually used only in the construction of traditional sailing ships. Maritime know-how was also needed to create the special curtains for the upstairs loft. Since the window is triangular, it was decided to commission a sailmaker to make a set of curtains that would function in the same way as a sail when raised and lowered. The crisscross pattern that distinguishes this window picks up on the theme of the nearby sheep-cote, which has a façade adorned with similar crisscross beams.

Most of the furniture has been specially made in the same oak as that used in the structure of the building. This includes the bed and the side table in the upstairs room, the sofas and sofa table on the ground floor, and the kitchen worktop and wooden surrounds. The kitchen appliances are by Bulthaup, while the tap is by Arne Jacobsen for Vola. The pendant lights over the kitchen worktop are by Dick Lundgren for the Stockholm-based company Men At Work. The garden furniture is also in oak and the tabletop is in grey limestone.

The Japanese-style garden was designed by the landscape company Nordisk Natur-Orienterad Design, which works closely with Wingårdh Arkitektkontor; the two companies share an office in Stockholm. The projecting screens are made from corded willow. The front of the house has sliding doors.

The sauna is the centre and the purpose of the Mill House. The curving bench is made of abachi wood, a hard version of balsa wood, which does not absorb heat, making it suitable to sit on. The walls of the sauna are, like most of the rest of the house, made from oak, while the floor is again in grey limestone. The traditional-looking sauna heater is Finnish – an example of the Finns' mastery of sauna equipment. The curving shower cubicle was constructed from stones cut in a triangular shape to make the curve of the wall smoother than they would have been if rectangular stones had been used.

OPPOSITE **The Karuselli chair by Yrjö Kukkapuro for Avarte from 1964 is the centrepiece of the living area. Its design is based on the idea of throwing yourself into the deep Finnish snow and letting your body shape the imprint. The sculpture is a plaster model for a larger sculpture by Oiva Olavi Waittinen.**

OPPOSITE **The Karuselli chair by Yrjö Kukkapuro for Avarte from 1964 is the centrepiece of the living area. Its design is based on the idea of throwing yourself into the deep Finnish snow and letting your body shape the imprint. The sculpture is a plaster model for a larger sculpture by Oiva Olavi Waittinen.**

ABOVE **The coffee table is custom-made by the design company NollaNolla, known for the interior of the trendy Helsinki restaurant Via. The wicker basket is made of willow. The rug is from IKEA. The light brown leather Wassily chairs by Marcel Breuer were designed in 1925 and are second-hand finds.**

HOUSE **ON STILTS**

The Finnish chef Aki Wahlman had this house on the large island of Kustavi designed by two architecture students, Kimmo Köpilä and Topi Laaksonen. The prefabricated house was built in two phases during 2004 and 2005. Wahlman himself designed the interior.

Aki Wahlman is a well-known name in Finland through his magic in the kitchen. He was rewarded as Chef of the Year in 1996; he has made five different television series since then, and has worked for various restaurants in Finland and Sweden. He is also a qualified teacher and has taught at Turku University of Applied Sciences. He lives just outside Turku on the west coast of Finland when he is not at his country home.

The house is called Villa Nina and the sauna building Rosa-Maria. The buildings are set on a large island in the north Turku archipelago, in the Baltic Sea. The surrounding

THIS PAGE The sauna building has a living room with a long narrow window that gives views of the sea so that after a sauna you can judge whether to throw yourself into the water or simply have a shower. The easy chairs are from IKEA but look distinctly Finnish in this setting.

countryside is covered with birch and fir trees and slopes gently down towards the sea. In common with most other beaches in Finland, the shore is covered with bare rock. During autumn and winter, the faraway lighthouse at Isokari can be seen blinking on the horizon. There is a sturdily built bridge by the water; the icy winters are notorious for taking with them any weak structures.

Rather than being set straight onto rocky ground, the house was mounted on steel and concrete pillars so that the impact on the ancient rocks below would be minimal. The main building materials are wood and glass. The façade is made from black-stained pine constructed according to a technique borrowed from Norway. Laid horizontally, it has open joints between the boards to allow air to circulate. The large glass surfaces are made from thick glass inserted straight into the load-bearing frames. The double-glazing consists of two 6 mm panes enclosing a gas that provides thermal insulation.

The main building is a rectangular U-shape, with the opening of the U facing inland, away from the wind. The living area is situated on the west, facing the setting sun, while the bedrooms are in their own wing on the eastern side. The roof is covered with untreated copper, and the same material has been used for gutters and water spouts.

ABOVE **Steel and concrete stilts were used to support the house so that the ancient rocks beneath it did not need to be built over. A walkway links the main building with the sauna house, and another walkway leads down to the bridge by the water. The surrounding birch and pine trees were carefully preserved during the building process. Seen from this angle, the house looks as if it has a flat roof, but it is actually sloping inwards, to drain away rain and snow.**

ABOVE, RIGHT AND OPPOSITE
The kitchen units, made specially for the house, are in walnut veneer; the dining table is also custom-made. The dark-stained interior wall extends into the exterior, blurring the boundary between inside and outside. While there are steps up to the kitchen, the ceiling height stays the same so that the living area at the back of the house is more intimate than at the front. The glass is inserted straight into the load-bearing frames; it has gas between the panes to supply thermal insulation.

LEFT Gaps have been left between the planks in the façade in order to allow daylight to penetrate into the semi-open atrium while it remains protected from the sea wind. The floorboards used throughout the house are made from 120 mm thick lacquered pine from Lapland. The pine has been coloured to match the larch used for the floor of the outdoor atrium.

ABOVE Suspended over the dining table are the famous Golden Bell brass pendant lights, designed by Alvar Aalto in the 1930s. The comfortable dining chairs are another Finnish design classic: the Kilta chair by Olli Mannermaa from 1955, recently put back into production by Martela. These particular chairs are originals that Wahlman had reupholstered.

Over time, the roof and gutters will take on a green patina. The roof slopes towards the inner courtyard at the centre of the U-shape to drain away rain and snow. Seen from a distance, the building gives the appearance of having a flat roof.

Since the floor is lower at the back of the house than at the front, while the roof and inner ceiling remain at the same level, there is an apparent variation in ceiling height that puts the emphasis on the front room with its spectacular views to the horizon, where passing ships can be seen. Outside is a terrace covered by the projecting roof, which gives protection from rain and wind. On the side of the building is a semi-open atrium for use on summer evenings.

The kitchen units are made from walnut veneer. The Skandic tap in the kitchen and other similar appliances in the house are by the 175-year-old Swedish company Gustavsberg. The dining table has been special made for the house. The brass lights over the dining table are the famous Golden Bell pendants, designed by Alvar Aalto; they were used both at Aalto's Savoy restaurant in Helsinki in 1937 and at his Poetry Room at Harvard University, USA, in 1948. The Golden Bell is no longer in production in this version, but Wahlman

THE U-SHAPED HOUSE IS ORIENTED WITH ITS BACK TO THE WIND. ITS LIVING AREA, ON THE WEST, FACES THE SETTING SUN; THE BEDROOMS HAVE THEIR OWN WING ON THE EASTERN SIDE.

OPPOSITE **In the large wood-fired sauna building, the seating is made from alder wood, which does not absorb heat as much as most other woods. Alder also gives off a pleasant natural scent when moist and warm. There is a metal bucket and scoop on the floor for throwing water onto the hot stones.**

ABOVE, RIGHT **The horizontal pine wall in the bedroom is black-stained, while the pine ceiling is light-stained to provide a distinct contrast. The bedspread is by the Swedish company Gant and the Kilta chair was designed by Olli Mannermaa in 1955.**

was lucky to find some made in the 1950s at a Helsinki café about to close down. The floor lights are also an Alvar Aalto design, called model A805 and designed by Aalto in 1953–54. They have a white-painted metal lampshade and a base and stand covered with black leather; the upper part is made of polished brass.

The comfortable dining chairs are another Finnish design classic, the Kilta chair by Olli Mannermaa from 1955. In its time, the Kilta was sold in great numbers across the world, and is even represented in the permanent collection of the Museum of Modern Art in New York. Martela, the largest Finnish office furniture company, has recently started to produce the chairs again. The Kilta chairs belonging to Aki Wahlman are original ones that he had reupholstered. They are used in several rooms.

The floor used throughout the inside of house is made from 120 mm thick lacquered pine from Lapland in northern Finland. The pine has been coloured to match the larch that was used to cover the outdoor terrace floor. In the bedroom, the horizontal pine wall has been stained black, while the ceiling, also made of pine, has been treated with a light stain to create a contrast and make the ceiling seem higher. In the wood-fired sauna building, alder wood was chosen for the seating because it absorbs less heat than most other woods. Alder also gives off a natural scent when moist and warm. The sauna walls are treated with a moisture-resistant stain.

SLEEK COUNTRY

The early 1930s saw the rapid absorption
into Scandinavian architecture of the
modernist style, which was perhaps more
eagerly embraced in Scandinavia than anywhere
else in Europe. The style was out of fashion during
the 1970s and 1980s, but has been enthusiastically
revived by a younger generation of architects,
this time with a more international influence.
Country houses are among the most prominent
representatives of this new modernism,
often renamed minimalism for a new era.

THIS PICTURE **The exterior is made of cedar wood, an unusual material for Scandinavian country homes but renowned for keeping off moisture and repelling insects. A flat roof might have caused problems in northern Scandinavia but in the southern Norwegian archipelago the winter winds are strong enough to prevent the snow from settling.**

WINDOW ON **NATURE**

Like the very best Cuban cigar boxes, this house is made from cedar wood to withstand moisture and insects. The house is also shaped like a box, but when deciding on the shape and positioning of the building the architects were sensitive to the natural setting.

The house is located within the Kragerø municipality, part of the county of Telemark, a region made famous in the 1965 film *The Heroes of Telemark*, starring Kirk Douglas and Richard Harris. Kragerø is between two and three hours' drive from Oslo and popular with summer visitors. In the summer, the inhabitants of Kragerø increase from 10,000 to about 50,000. The Kragerø coastline has 495 islands, the most visited of which is Jomfruland, or the Virgin Island.

ABOVE **The house is constructed over one floor and the roof is one, almost continuous line, but it rises up on the eastern side, following the contours of the land.**

LEFT **Kragerø has a long seafaring history; by 1875, its fleet consisted of 170 ships and 1,614 seamen. Among the city's visitors was Edvard Munch, who settled there in 1909.**

<< WHILE THE EXTERIOR IS MADE OF CEDAR, THE WALLS AND CEILINGS ARE MADE OF ASPEN, AND THE FLOORS BOTH INSIDE AND OUT ARE OAK. THE AIM WAS TO COMBINE THE VARIOUS >> WOODS IN ONE UNIFIED LOOK. >>

The house was designed by the renowned Norwegian architects' firm of Lund Hagem, owned by Svein Lund and Einar Hagem, which employs some 30 staff. The distinctive aspects of Lund Hagem's work include a commitment to the preservation of existing natural features and an emphasis on choosing sympathetic materials. Both aspects are evident in this house. Lund Hagem started by working on residential projects but have moved into major cultural and commercial buildings over the last few years. The summerhouse for the Norwegian royal family is one of their most prestigious projects.

Set on an island accessible only by boat, the house was completed in 2005 and covers about 125 square metres. In Norway the size of any new structure, particularly on the coast, is strictly controlled by building regulations. To make the most of the space available, the architects worked with the decked outdoor areas.

Rather than using the same wood throughout, it was decided to incorporate several different woods in the construction of the house. The thinking behind this was that different woods react differently to

THIS PICTURE AND LEFT **The rocky ground on which the house stands is higher at the eastern end of the site, so the architects decided to raise the floor level slightly in that section, and to create a semi-enclosed space for the library. Inside, they positioned a large fireplace with** openings on two sides, onto the main area and the library area; the two separate chimneys serving this fireplace are a distinctive design feature of the building. While the library is enclosed behind the fireplace, it has an abundance of natural daylight from a skylight in the roof.

LEFT The window frames are all made of wood. Steel frames are not a realistic option in a house so close to the ocean. The alternative would be aluminium, but aluminium has little of the tactile structure and look of wooden frames.

RIGHT The architects decided not to follow the usual practice of building the outdoor decking along the house. Instead, the decking juts out at a 90-degree angle.

BELOW The inside of the house is sparsely furnished. The kitchen units are by Bulthaup and the large dining table is specially made for the house. The chairs are by Vitra.

changing temperatures and humidity depending on whether they are inside or outside. So, while the exterior of the house is made of cedar, the walls and ceilings are made of aspen, and the floors both inside and outside are made of oak. The aim was to combine the different woods into one unified look.

The window frames are all wooden, a feature that is quite unusual in modern buildings. Lacquered-steel frames would not have been an option in a house so close to the ocean since salt-water winds would have corroded the steel. The alternative was aluminium, the most common material used for windows today, but aluminium has little of the tactile structure and look of wood. The need for maintenance might be higher, but this is compensated for by the visual impact.

The house consists of one single space, but the rocky ground called for a raised section at the eastern end. Rather than blasting

the rocks away, the architects decided to raise the floor level slightly in that section, and to create a semi-enclosed space for a library. Inside, they positioned a large fireplace with openings both onto the main area and onto the library area; this arrangement requires two separate chimneys – a distinctive design feature that affects the look of the whole building. While the library is enclosed behind the large fireplace, it has an abundance of natural daylight from a skylight in the roof.

Water flanks the house on both sides, with the eastern side facing the ocean and the prevailing winds. On the western side, where the summer sun does not set until about 11 p.m., rocks provide some shelter from the wind.

The architects decided not to build the outdoor decking alongside the house in the usual fashion. Instead, the decking juts out at a 90-degree angle from the house, towards the sheltering rocks. This creates an outdoor atrium that can be used even when the wind is blowing, and the sea is visible to the east through an open glass façade. Instead of cutting down a mature tree that was in the way of the decking, the architects incorporated the tree into the plan by making a hole for it. This is typical of Lund Hagem's work.

FAR RIGHT **With its spectacular views of the skerries, the living area constitutes the most dramatic part of the whole building.**

INSET **The bedroom is much more private than the rest of the house. A steel window frame was installed to contain and stabilize the huge expanse of glass.**

BELOW **The washbasin beside the window is as exposed to public view as most of the rest of the interior. The trunks of the trees outside are as straight as the raisers of the window frame inside.**

« BY 1875 KRAGERØ WAS THE SIXTH LARGEST MARITIME TOWN IN NORWAY, WITH A FLEET OF 170 SHIPS. IT HAS LONG ATTRACTED NOTABLE VISITORS, INCLUDING THE PAINTER EDVARD MUNCH, WHO SETTLED THERE IN 1909. »

The inside of the house is sparsely furnished. The semi-freestanding kitchen includes Bulthaup units and the large dining table is custom-made for the house. The bedroom is different from the rest of the building in that it is not surrounded by glass, but instead kept very private. For the bedroom window, the architects chose a steel, rather than wooden, frame to contain the large expanse of glass. The living area has a clear view over the skerries outside and is perhaps the most dramatic part of the whole building. The black window frame reinforces its Norse name origin. The English word 'window' is based on the Norse words 'wind' and 'eye', and this is really what the architects have created: an eye for the wind. They admit that the design of this particular opening was inspired by the Mallorca home of Jørn Ützon, the Danish architect of the Sydney Opera House.

BOXING **CLEVER**

Light is everything in Scandinavia and this house has been built to admit as much of it as possible. Rather than imposing itself on nature, the house looks as though it has grown out of the soil, and the glass in the windows reflects the trees and fields nearby.

THIS PICTURE **The classic 3107 chairs, designed by Arne Jacobsen, and made by the company Fritz Hansen since 1955, are paired with a white B412 span-leg table, designed by the Dane Piet Hein and the Swede Bruno Mathsson in 1966, also made by Fritz Hansen. So popular is this combination of chairs and table that many believe they are by the same designer.**

≪ THE CONSPICUOUS FEATURE IS THE BLACK EXTERIOR. THIS ISN'T ABOUT PRETTY RURAL HOMES THAT RELY HEAVILY ON TRADITION. THE HOUSES ARE CLEARLY SCANDINAVIAN IN THEIR APPEARANCE, BUT FIRMLY ROOTED IN MODERN ≫ ARCHITECTURE.

OPPOSITE, BELOW **The black-stained larch wall behind the iron fireplace gives the impression that the soot from the fireplace has darkened the wall over the years, which is what would have happened if there were natural wood on this wall. In the rest of the house, the larch cladding on the walls and floors has been kept in its original light colour to contrast with the black-stained spruce exterior.**

OPPOSITE, ABOVE LEFT AND RIGHT **The bathtub has built-in air and water massage features, and the bathroom floor and WC both have underfloor heating. As in the rest of the house, the bedroom walls are all clad in horizontal strips of larch. Doorframes and thresholds are also made from solid larch. All door handles are in stainless steel; brass or plastic would be completely out of character with the building.**

Schmidt Hammer Lassen, the most prominent Danish architectural firm since the heyday of Arne Jacobsen in the mid-20th century, have designed 12 houses in Birkeengen in northern Denmark. Run by Morten Schmidt, Bjarne Hammer, John Lassen, Kim Holst Jensen and Morten Holm, the practice has worked in many countries other than Denmark, including Norway, Sweden, Iceland, the Faeroe Islands, Greenland, France, Monaco, Spain, Germany, Belgium, Luxembourg, Poland, Saudi Arabia, Dubai and the USA. The architects might not put themselves on the same level as Jacobsen, but they are without doubt the most celebrated practice in Denmark today, and they follow in Jacobsen's modernist footsteps.

Schmidt Hammer Lassen has a philosophical, almost poetical view of architecture, describing its purpose as: 'To organize the setting of life and expression, not for the sake of form but for the interaction between light, colours and texture. This interaction creates space. To create space is to create identities, and to create identities is to create fixed points for the reality and existence of man.' The Birkeengen development is the physical realization of this theory, as interpreted in simple country houses rather than a grand project.

The 12 houses were planned for a very specific location; Birkeengen lies in the beautiful Rågeleje area, perhaps the most attractive part of the northern Danish coast. The ocean is only some 1,200 metres away, and while the area has little traffic, it is not far from Copenhagen. The popular Heather Hill area is also nearby, with golf or walks in the forest as attractive alternatives to staying at home. There are also several restaurants nearby.

Each house occupies 130 square metres, with an outdoor terrace of 45 square metres and a garage of 35 square metres with room for garden tools and other accessories. The most conspicuous feature is the black exterior; this development is not about pretty country homes that rely heavily on tradition. The houses are undoubtedly Scandinavian in their appearance, but firmly

rooted in modern architecture. Priority is given to considerations of functionality, quality, human scale and simplicity – all prominent features of modern Scandinavian architecture.

The exterior walls of each house are clad in horizontal planks of black-stained spruce. Inside, the main material is larch, used to make the walls and main floors; only the areas between the windows have been black-stained, otherwise the light, natural colour of the larch has been retained. Even the garage is made from spruce, with a light larch interior.

The inside space is planned so that the living room, kitchen and terrace are part of the front, higher area while the three bedrooms, the WC and bathroom are part of the lower back area. The large glass frontage means the living area appears to be continuous with the outside terrace. There is a loft of 11 square metres above the kitchen. A playful little window has been added at the side, acting like a small framed picture of nature.

The roof is covered in black roof paper, with edges in black-lacquered zinc and aluminium. The slanted roof is not only an attractive design feature but also necessary for dealing with winter snowfall. Having perfectly horizontal roofs was a dream of Scandinavia's modernist architects in the 20th century, but it became an expensive experiment for many house-owners once the snow started to fall and build up its crushing weight. Past generations had dealt with the problem by constructing steeply slanted roofs – but a steep slant would have made it impossible to create the magnificent ceiling height in these new buildings.

The main theme running through all the houses is the sharp contrast between the black elements of the façade and the natural-coloured wood, a contrast underlined by the use of black furniture. The freestanding iron fireplace with its exposed chimney pipe that continues up through the roof is a typical Danish feature; such a device was used for centuries to warm simple fishermen's huts but is equally suitable in modern architecture.

OPPOSITE, ABOVE AND BELOW The elegant Vola tap by Arne Jacobsen from 1967 is a design classic not only in Denmark; it is nowadays seen all over the world. The outdoor furniture is the Ocean series by Hans Thyge Raunkjær for Trip Trap.

THIS PAGE A steep, white-painted staircase leads up to the loft. The stainless-steel vacuum jug with black handle is by Erik Magnussen from 1977 for Stelton. The white kitchen bar top is made from glass. Most appliances are by Bauknecht.

THIS PAGE **The long dining table is a design by Claesson Koivisto Rune to the owners' specifications. The chairs are heirlooms, which nicely complement the strict table design. The installation of the sliding-glass wall was one of the few alterations made to the old school house.**

ABOVE AND ABOVE RIGHT **The daybed, made to the owners' design, is intended for the comfort of anyone who wants to have a rest while the other is busy in the kitchen next door. The floor lamp is by Arne Jacobsen, designed in 1958. The floorboards are the originals, brought back to life.**

GENIUS IN **GLASS**

Glass and ceramics designer Ingegerd Råman, who has become something of an institution in Sweden, treasures her country house in Skåne as a place for both winding down and creating. Originally a school, it is now a study in contemporary Swedish minimalism.

When Ingegerd Råman and her partner, Claes, bought their house on Österlen in the southern Swedish province of Skåne, it was essentially an untouched 1920s school building. Little of the original floor plan with its two large teaching rooms has been changed, except for the removal of some internal doors and partitions. All the original floorboards were kept, even though a great deal of love and attention was required to restore them to their former glory.

Claes did most of the building work himself and acted as a self-appointed site foreman. The entire job was completed in only four months. This included the painstaking renovation of the large windows; both of the owners were determined not to replace them with modern copies in suspect materials.

The collaboration with the young but successful architectural trio of Mårten Claesson, Eero Koivisto and Ola Rune was crucial to the

BELOW **The schoolhouse was built in 1925, just before modernism transformed Swedish architecture. After the school closed down, it was used as a community centre until Ingegerd and Claes bought and renovated it. Its ceiling soars to a magnificent height, and the sight lines goes right through the house.**

OPPOSITE, ABOVE LEFT **The all-concealing white kitchen is by Saari, a small Finnish kitchen company popular among modern Swedish architects. The bar stools, by Alvar Aalto, were bought by Ingegerd in the 1960s.**

OPPOSITE, ABOVE RIGHT **The fireplace in the corner is a Swedish tile stove, famous for its superior heat distribution. This one was made in Karlskrona in 1925, but was put in by Ingegerd and Claes. The chaise longue is by Källemo.**

OPPOSITE, BELOW **On the kitchen work surface is some of Ingegerd Råman's latest works in etched black glass for Orrefors.**

THIS PICTURE **The desk, whose inlaid-leather top is new, came from an old Swedish castle. The chair is an auction find; the table light is by Arne Jacobsen from 1958.**

success of the project. In Sweden, Ingegerd Råman is the queen of modern, uncompromising, simple glass, while the architects are the champions of minimalist architecture and furniture design. They all share a passion for Japanese aesthetics and the limited colour palette of black and white; the architects are even described as the 'Men in Black', while she is rarely seen in any other colour.

Even in her early work in the 1960s, Råman turned against waves of colours and wild patterns. 'My work has always represented a link between simplicity, function and aesthetic values,' she says. In 1995, she was made Professor of Honour by the Swedish government, and was awarded the Prince Eugen Medal by the King of Sweden in 1998. One of her recent commissions was for a new heraldic symbol of the Kingdom of Sweden for the Swedish parliament, placed behind the Speaker of the House. She has made stainless-steel cutlery for the Swedish company Gense, and ceramics for the Norwegian company Figgjo and Sweden's Gustavsberg.

Just beside the old house stands a modern white cube, 5 metres high and with a slanted roof, which was designed by Claesson Koivisto Rune. This is Ingegerd Råman's ceramics studio. Råman does not particularly like to be referred to by the title 'designer' — even though she is a brilliant one — and prefers to called a 'ceramicist' since ceramics

involves working with the hands. To describe the white cube as her design studio would upset her; on the contrary, it is her ceramics workshop. She creates by stretching the limit of the materials she works with. This has included the rediscovery of 1920s and 1930s techniques of etching, but using totally modern patterns. She experiments by marking the glass with grinders and files, and consults glassblowers about what can be done.

Although she trained as a ceramicist, it is through her work in glass that Råman has attained commercial success and fame. She first worked for

THIS PICTURE The 1930s Tank chair by Alvar Aalto, upholstered in black wool, is not only seriously stylish but also very comfortable. Behind it sits glass by (from left to right) Per Sundberg, Ingegerd Råman and Ingeborg Lundin, all for Orrefors.

the small but old and well-respected Johansfors and Skruf glassworks in the 'glass country' of Småland in southern Sweden, a couple of hours from her present country home. At Skruf, she made official glassware for the Swedish parliament, the foreign office and several Swedish embassies. She joined Orrefors, the most revered of the Swedish glassworks, in 1999. There she has created, and continues to create, a succession of simple but exquisite bowls, vases and glasses. Her work is represented in numerous international museum collections and has been shown in many exhibitions both in Sweden and abroad.

The country house in Skåne is a clear extension of her and Claes's aesthetics. Many of the pieces – not that there are very many – are what you would expect in a trendy Scandinavian house: some Aalto, some Jacobsen, some Kjaerholm. But when you speak to Råman, she says, 'The Alvar Aalto bar stools – yes, we bought them in the late 1960s. The Jacobsen Ant chair – I think Claes brought that with him when we met.' It is the same with her work. Some have criticized her for following trends, but her work has been as it is now for years; she arrived at her simple, monochrome aesthetic when most other people

were choosing shades of brown and yellow for their flower patterns. At the same time, she knows which glass designers she likes and says so. Perhaps surprisingly, she has always been a supporter of Per Sundberg, even though he brought something of punk rock design into traditional Swedish glass.

Beside Ingegerd and Claes's bed is Äpplet (the Apple vase) by Ingeborg Lundin, an icon of Swedish glass design from Orrefors, shaped like the Beatles' apple but made a decade before the Fab Four adopted the symbol. Äpplet is one of the most sought-after and collectable of all Swedish glass designs – Ingegerd's work excluded.

THIS PICTURE **Ingegerd and Claes designed the bed, and the long sideboard is designed by Claesson Koivisto Rune. The light is the British Bestlite from the 1930s. In front of the bed is a Japanese-inspired installation.**

THIS PICTURE **The Suppanen house is a real rural retreat, far away from neighbours and modern conveniences. Yet, the architect behind it has created a contemporary haven in the middle of the Baltic Sea. In true Finnish tradition, the surrounding woods are both outside and inside – acting as a constant reminder of where you are.**

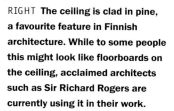
RIGHT **The ceiling is clad in pine, a favourite feature in Finnish architecture. While to some people this might look like floorboards on the ceiling, acclaimed architects such as Sir Richard Rogers are currently using it in their work.**

PRACTICAL **CHIC**

It is on a remote island, it stands on a rock and it is modern. But it is not part of a James Bond film set; it is simply a summerhouse by the Finnish architect and designer Ilkka Suppanen. If you look closely, it is even traditional – as long as you like Finnish modern.

The Suppanen house – called Villa Ilo – is in the Åland archipelago, between Finland and Sweden, and is reached from the harbour city of Turku in western Finland. The area is popular with sailors and visitors alike, but, although it is a haven in summer, the winters can be very demanding. Villa Ilo is unique in its curving form, which was designed to follow the shape of the land and complement the clifftop location. The house was built for relatives of the architect and designer Ilkka Suppanen.

Suppanen studied architecture at the Technical University of Helsinki, and interior and furniture design at the University of Art and Design Helsinki. In 1995, he founded Studio Suppanen in Helsinki. His clients include Artek, Axis, Cappellini, Ferlea, Lucente, Luhta, Nokia, Proventus and Saab. He was also one of the founders of the Snowcrash collective. Suppanen was rewarded in 2006 with the Bruno Mathsson prize, the most prestigious design award in Sweden. The Villa Ilo is one of his most recent projects.

The Suppanen house is on its own island, which takes about 20 minutes to reach by boat from the nearest inhabited island. It could be described as a typical Finnish summerhouse when it comes to its appliances and equipment, in that it has neither running water nor an electric cable to the mainland; the electricity supply is created by a system of solar panels. Instead, the house is self-sufficient and reliant on what the natural world around it can provide. When asked whether the house is typically Finnish, the architect Ilkka Suppanen simply answers, 'The house is in the middle of nature and, once you are there, you are part of the nature. But is this really Finnish? I do not really think of this once I am designing something.'

LEFT **The pine ceiling curves around the whole house, sucking in the chimney tops from the kitchen and fireplace. The kitchen is nothing out of the ordinary; haute cuisine is not a priority among Finnish country house owners.**

BELOW **The dining tables and chairs are by Alvar Aalto, designed in the 1930s.**

OPPOSITE **The fireplace with its concrete bench projecting left from the roaring fire, is one of the best features of the house. It was built by the present owners, and is extremely heavy. Note the simple, functional firewood basket.**

>> IT COULD BE DESCRIBED AS A TYPICAL FINNISH SUMMERHOUSE IN THAT IT HAS NEITHER RUNNING WATER NOR AN ELECTRICITY CABLE TO THE MAINLAND. INSTEAD, THE VILLA IS SELF-SUFFICIENT AND RELIANT ON WHAT THE NATURAL WORLD AROUND CAN PROVIDE. >>

Set on the highest point of the island, the building has a curved form that follows the contour of the rocky landscape. The ideal location for the villa was precisely calculated; it is oriented to take advantage of the sun's path and nature's diurnal rhythm. The site needed to offer protection from the prevailing Baltic winds, since the weather in this area can be fierce all year round. The house offers wonderful sea views and has plenty of attractive rock formations nearby, which is typical of the Åland archipelago. The potential difficulties presented by a site in such a steep spot were evident to Suppanen, but it he felt that it added to the drama of the house.

The house's area is 85 square metres and the sauna beside it covers 25 square metres. Proportionately, this might seem like a generous allocation of space for the sauna, but it is perfectly normal for a Finnish house. Indeed, a Finnish country house without a sauna is considered not only poor but bordering on the suspect. The choice is between an electric sauna (common in the city) and a traditional wood-fired sauna, like the one installed here. The effect of an electric

THIS PICTURE, INSET AND RIGHT
The sleeping section can be closed off by a large, sliding door fixed to a wooden beam in the ceiling. The bed area is close to one of the fireplaces, making it warm and comfortable. Visible just outside – like a snapshot of nature – is the untamed pine forest. The benches by the foot of the bed are by Alvar Aalto for Artek. The woven firewood basket made of birch can be found in farmers' markets across Finland.

sauna is considered to be totally different from that of a wood-fired sauna, with a much more intense experience to be had from a wood-fired version. The sauna is sited on a flat area near the tip of a headland, where it is exposed to winds nearly all the time. To minimize erosion, a large terrace has been laid around the sauna building. The dressing room, washroom and sauna itself are separated by glass partitions to create an feeling of one simple space. Steam generated by bathing in the sauna and washing steams up the glass partitions and provides privacy.

The choice of pine as the building material is, in the words of the architect, 'a very practical solution' – a comment that exemplifies the Finnish attitude not only to building but also to life in general. This intensely practical approach does not stop there. The house was built by just two men, the father and son who planned to live there, so it was crucial that none of the construction elements exceeded the maximum weight that could be carried by two people.

It took some effort to acquire building permission. The authorities were concerned that the house would be visible from the sea, so Suppanen experimented with various alternatives and produced a large number of drawings to convince them that this would not be a problem. A local contractor built the kitchen to Suppanen's brief, while the father and son owners constructed the fireplace. The bench was also built by the owners to Suppanen's design; it is made of concrete and covered by black glass plates. The furniture includes Finnish classics: Alvar Aalto tables, stools and chairs by Artek, the Harri Koskinen K chair for Woodnotes, and traditional firewood baskets.

A home away from home doesn't have to mean compromising on comfort and convenience when Danish design is involved. Mikkel Frost, Carsten Primdahl and Kolja Nielsen of the architectural firm 3XN have created a series of country houses for the Lübker golf resort at Djursland on Jutland in collaboration with the developer M2. The 3XN style is distinguished by clean lines and crystalline forms.

BLACK & **WHITE**

THIS PICTURE **In Danish homes, there is always room for two design abbreviations: AJ (for Arne Jacobsen) and B&O (for Bang & Olufsen). Here, the two icons are represented by the chairs, and the television and sound system. The unusual candleholders are called Kubus and were designed by the Danish architect Mogens Lassen in 1960 as a reaction against the over-ornate candleholders common at the time. The freestanding fireplace is also typically Danish.**

Developers of large-scale housing schemes have generally done the world few architectural favours, whatever country they have been active in. Keeping costs low is always one of their top priorities, and they will tend to choose an uncontroversial architectural style that will suit as many people as possible. Recently, however, there has been a growing realization that, while we might not all be seriously wealthy, the appreciation of good architecture is not confined to the rich. In some countries, the more far-sighted developers have hired the services of skilled and highly acclaimed architects. The work of M2 in Denmark is a good example of this trend.

M2 decided to collaborate with architectural practices that would not normally work on mass-produced houses, and aim for a higher standard of building than would be usual in mass housing. This was not a particularly revolutionary move; it was just that few people had done it before. In fact, it is very similar to building any ordinary house; you have to choose from a number of standard builds. The difference is that all the houses on offer are of high architectural quality.

An example of such a collaborative venture is M2's development of the Lübker golf resort in Denmark. Golf may be regarded by some as a pastime for the rich, but in Scandinavia it is fast becoming a sport for all and overtaking football as a participation sport. Almost everyone, young or old, plays golf today, as long as there is no snow on the ground.

For the Lübker golf resort, M2 worked with three architects' offices; CEBRA, Schmidt Hammer Lassen and 3XN. The golf course itself was designed by Robert Trent Jones II. It consists of three 9-hole courses in a clover shape with the clubhouse at the centre, making 27 holes in total. The whole Lübker golf resort area covers some 171 hectares and is located on Djursland in Jutland.

Danish country houses are no longer the small, simple, unheated structures with tar-covered roof paper they used to be; nowadays they are often as well equipped as any city villa. The three architectural practices involved presented three entirely different designs. Mikkel Frost, Carsten Primdahl and Kolja Nielsen from the large firm 3XN contributed with the KipUp House. The original name of the firm was

3 X Nielsen (the most common surname in Denmark) after the founder Kim Herforth Nielsen. As the company grew and included people with other surnames, it was shortened to 3XN. Today, they have offices in both Aarhus and Copenhagen. Among their most prestigious projects are the Museum of Liverpool and the Arts and Media centre at Salford University. They are also behind the new football stadium in Horsens, Denmark, replacing an old stadium that was large enough to attract both Madonna and the Rolling Stones. They have also designed the Danish embassy in Berlin, part of the joint Scandinavian embassy.

The KipUp house is an altogether smaller project. Its total area is only 100 square metres, while the outside terrace is 27 square metres, all on one level. It has three bedrooms but, rather than the classic form of room division, it has flexible walls that can be moved to adapt to changing needs. A long wooden bench extends along a wall throughout the entire house, and continues onto the outside terrace to blur the border between inside and outside. There is a loft in the main room that can also be used for sleeping. The kitchen is discreetly integrated into the wall of the living room and has been placed close to the entrance to the terrace in order to facilitate outdoor eating.

All appliances and materials are of the best quality; the floor is Douglas pine from Dinesen; the bathroom appliances are by Philippe Starck for Duravit; and the stainless-steel bathroom accessories are by Knud Holscher for the Danish

company D-line. The house is fitted with a security system that can be remotely controlled from a mobile telephone or laptop computer. Even the heating can be remotely controlled. The timber façade has been stained black, while the terrace and the projecting bench have been left in their natural colours to provide a striking contrast. The shape is like a crystal, with triangular windows, projecting corners and slanting roof sections.

The furniture and accessories are what could be called the new Danish Modern; a mixture of Italian contemporary and Danish classic design. Black 3107 chairs by Arne Jacobsen from Fritz Hansen, music and television system by Bang & Olufsen, and outdoor furniture from the Ocean series by the Danish firm Trip Trap are combined with the Spun desk light by Sebastian Wrong and the Romeo floor lamp by Philippe Starck, both for Flos.

THIS PICTURE **Danish country houses are no longer the simple structures with tar-covered roof paper that they used to be; today they are often as well equipped as any city villa. The kitchen at the KipUp house is sited close to the terrace to facilitate outdoor dining.**

ABOVE **The timber façade has been stained black, while the terrace and projecting bench have been left in their natural colours to provide a striking contrast. The shape of the house is distinctly crystalline, with triangular windows, projecting corners and slanting roof sections.**

SUPPLIERS

Aram
110 Drury Lane
Covent Garden
London WC2B 5SG
020 7557 7557
www.aram.co.uk
One of the first UK retailers of modern design.

Area
13–15 Grand Arcade
New Briggate
Leeds LS1 6PG
0113 228 2605
www.area-uk.com
Jacob Jensen, Normann Copenhagen and Verner Panton chairs.

Atomic Interiors
Plumtree Square
Nottingham NG1 1JF
0115 941 5577
www.atomicinteriors.co.uk
Top dog in Nottingham for modern design.

Back2myplace
Cardiff, Wales (currently relocating in Cardiff)
02920 514093
www.b2mp.com
Contract dealer and retailer for major brands such as Fritz Hansen and Knoll.

Boom!
53 Chalk Farm Road
London NW1 8AN
020 7284 4622
Retro plastic furniture and lighting as well as original glass and textiles.

Cale Shiang Partnership
58–62 Holywell Hill
St Albans
Hertfordshire AL11BX
08702 202055
A wide selection of Hans Wegner and Bruno Mathsson furniture.

Central
33–35 Little Clarendon Street
Oxford OX1 2HU
01865 311141
Arne Jacobsen and Verner Panton furniture.

Century
68 Marylebone High Street
London W1 3AQ
020 7487 5100
Vintage furniture and objects.

Co-existence
288 Upper Street
London N1 2TZ
020 7354 8817
www.coexistence.co.uk
Mainly a contract showroom.

The Conran Shop
81 Fulham Road
London SW3 6RD
020 7589 74041
www.conran.com
Changing selection of modern designs from around the world.

DesignShopUK
116 Causewayside
Edinburgh EH9 1PU
0131 667 7078
www.designshopuk.com
Wide selection of gifts and furniture.

Fandango
17 Essex Road
London N1 2SE
020 7689 8778
Vintage furniture and objects, including Danish glass and lighting.

Fusion
30 Church Street
Birmingham B3 2NP
0121 2361020
www.fusionlifestyle.co.uk
Interior lifestyle store selling Marimekko and other Scandinavian brands.

Great Danes
12 Connaught Avenue
Frinton-on-sea
Essex CO13 9PW
01255 852285
Various Scandinavian brands.

The Home
Salt Mills
Victoria Road, Saltaire
Bradford BD18 3LB
01274 530770
A good selection of Scandinavian design, with an emphasis on Finnish design.

IKEA
255 North Circular Road
London NW13 0JQ
020 8208 5600
And stores nationwide
www.ikea.com
The PS collection is worth a look for slightly more cutting-edge designs from this Swedish giant.

Inhouse
28 Howe Street
Edinburgh EH3 6TG
0131 225 2888
(also branch in Glasgow)
Mainly accessories, some from Iittala and Stelton.

Loft
24–28 Dock Street
Leeds LS10 1JF
0113 305 1515
British, Italian and Scandinavian products.

Luna
23 George Street
Nottingham NG1 3BH
0115 924 3267
Vintage glass, ceramics and lighting, including many Scandinavian pieces.

Marimekko
16–17 St Christopher's Place
London W1U 1NZ
020 7486 6454
Fabrics, clothing, and kitchen, bedroom and bathroom accessories from this iconic brand.

Origin 101
Gateway Arcade
Islington High Street
London N1 0PY
07747 758852
www.origin101.co.uk
Vintage furniture and accessories.

Overdose on Design
182 Brick Lane
London E1 6SP
020 7613 1266
Vintage furniture and accessories.

Paere Dansk
13 Stratford Road Kensington
London W8 6RF
07771 861 939
www.paeredansk.com
Vintage Danish design.

Places and Spaces
30 Old Town, Clapham
London SW4 0LB
020 7498 0998
www.placesandspaces.com
A mixture of modern furniture and accessories.

Planet Bazaar
149 Drummond Street
London NW1 2PB
020 7387 832
Some Danish glass and furniture.

SCP
135–139 Curtain Road
London EC2A 3BX
020 7739 1869
www.scp.co.uk
Changing selection of modern design from around the world.

Shannon
68 Walcot Street
Bath BA1 5BD
01225 424 222
A good selection of Marimekko and Iittala, and furniture by designers such as Hans Wegner and Bruno Mathsson.

Sigmar London
263 Kings Road
London SW3 5EL
020 7751 5801
www.sigmarlondon.com
Vintage furniture, mainly Danish.

Simply Scandinavian
6 Eggars Hill
Aldershot
Hampshire GU11 3NQ
01252 334499
Gifts and lighting.

Skandium
86 Marylebone High Street
London W1U 4QS
245-249 Brompton Road
London SW3 2EP
020 7935 2077
www.skandium.com
The single largest retailer of original Scandinavian design in the UK, representing anyone who is anyone in the field. Furniture, lighting, textiles, glassware, crockery, cutlery, books and gifts from small and large manufacturers in Denmark, Finland, Norway and Sweden. Both design classics and modern designs.

Snowhome
42 Gillygate
York YO31 7EQ
01904671155
www.snow-home.co.uk
Lighting and gift items.

Tangram
33/37 Jeffrey Street
Edinburgh EH1 1DH
0131 556 6551
Mainly a contract showroom but welcoming to the public. Scandinavian products include Gärsnäs and Lammhults furniture, along with Woodnotes rugs and blinds.

Themes and Variations
231 Westbourne Grove
London W11 2SE
020 7727 5531
www.themesand variations.co.uk
Exclusive selection of vintage design, with a particular focus on Danish furniture.

Tom Tom
42 New Compton Street
London WC2H 8DA
020 7240 7909
Great for vintage furniture.

Tony Walker Interiors
Whitehall Court
14 Telford Road
Edinburgh EH4 2BD
0131 343 6151
www.tonywalkerinteriors.com
Mainly a contract showroom but welcoming to the public.

Twentytwentyone
274 Upper Street
London N1 2UA
020 7288 1996
www.twentytwentyone.co.uk
Good selection of new and vintage accessories and furniture, including pieces by Artek, Rosendahl and Stelton.

Utility
86 Bold Street
Liverpool L1 4HY
0151 707 9919
Best design shop in Liverpool.

Vessel
114 Kensington Park Road
London W11 2PW
020 7727 8001
Focusing mainly on new Italian and Scandinavian glass and ceramics, this shop has an excellent collection of investment pieces.

Vitra
30 Clerkenwell Road
London EC1M 5PQ
020 7608 6200
www.vitra.com
Manufacturer of several classic Verner Panton designs that are now back in production.

PICTURE CREDITS

All photography by Paul Ryan unless otherwise stated.   Key: ph = photographer, a = above, b = below, l = left, r = right, c = centre.

Endpapers the summer house of Peter Morgan at the Bjäte peninsula (in the northwest of Scania); **page 1** a house designed by Schmidt Hammer Lassen, developer Birkeengen Aps, Denmark – www.birkeengen.dk/ph Sus Rosenquist; **2** a house designedby Ilkka Suppanen in Finland; **3** the home of Ingegerd Raman and Claes Söderquist in Sweden; **3 inset** Ritva Puotila's summer home in Finland; **4–5** the home of Ingegerd Raman and Claes Söderquist in Sweden; **6** the summer home of Elina Helenius and Mika Mahlberg in Finland; **7** Ritva Puotila's summer home in Finland; **8–9** the home of Nils Tunebjer in Sweden; **10b** Ritva Puotila's summer home in Finland; **11b** the home of Nils Tunebjer in Sweden; **12al** the summer house of Mikko Pulkkinen in Kustovi, Finland (built in 1967); **12ar** the summer home of Elina Helenius and Mika Mahlberg in Finland; **12b** the home of Jette Riis and Lars Hansen on Rømø Island, Denmark/ph Sus Rosenquist; **13a** Aki Wahlman's summer home in Finland; **13b** the summer house of the Engh family on the southern coast of Norway; **14** Ritva Puotila's summer home in Finland; **15al** the summer house of the Engh family on the southern coast of Norway; **15ar** Ritva Puotila's summer home in Finland; **16l** a house designed by Ilkka Suppanen in Finland; **16r–17l** the summer house of Peter Morgan at the Bjäte peninsula (in the northwest of Scania); **17ar** summer house at Hvasser belonging to Astir Eidsbo and Tore Lindholm; **17br** the summer house of the Engh family on the southern coast of Norway; **18–19** M2/ph Sus Rosenquist; **19r** a house designed by Schmidt Hammer Lassen, developer Birkeengen Aps, Denmark – www.birkeengen.dk/ph Sus Rosenquist; **20l** Ritva Puotila's summer home in Finland; **20b** summer house at Hvasser belonging to Astir Eidsbo and Tore Lindholm; **22al&r** Ritva Puotila's summer home in Finland; **22ac** Aki Wahlman's summer home in Finland; **33b** the home of Ingegerd Raman and Claes Söderquist in Sweden;**23** the summer house of Peter Morgan at the Bjäte peninsula (in the northwest of Scania); **24** the home of Jette Riis and Lars Hansen on Rømø Island, Denmark/ph Sus Rosenquist; **25b** the home of Ingegerd Raman and Claes Söderquist's home in Sweden; **26–27** a house designed by Ilkka Suppanen in Finland; **38–45** the home of Jette Riis and Lars Hansen on Rømø Island, Denmark/ph Sus Rosenquist; **46–51** the home of Nils Tunebjer in Sweden; **54–61** Ritva Puotila's summer home in Finland; **62–67** the summer house of Mikko Pulkkinen in Kustovi, Finland (built in 1967); **74–81** summer houseat Hvasser belonging to Astir Eidsbo and Tore Lindholm; **84–89** the summer home of Elina Helenius and Mika Mahlberg in Finland; **90–97** the summer house of Peter Morgan at the Bjäte peninsula (in the northwest ofScania); **98–105** Aki Wahlman's summer home in Finland; **108–15** the summer house of the Engh family on the southern coast of Norway; **116–21** house designed by Schmidt Hammer Lassen, developer Birkeengen Aps, Denmark – www.birkeengen.dk/ph Sus Rosenquist; **122–27** the home of Ingegerd Raman and Claes Söderquist in Sweden; **128–33** a house designed by Ilkka Suppanen in Finland; **134–39** M2/ph Sus Rosenquist.

BUSINESS CREDITS

Claesson Koivisto Rune Arkitektkontor
Sankt Paulsgatan 25
SE-118 48 Stockholm
Sweden
T: + 46 8 644 58 63
F: + 46 8 644 58 83
Pages 3, 4–5, 22b, 25b, 122–27.

Studio Elina Helenius
Orioninkatu 10-12,
00550 Helsinki
Finland
mail@elinahelenius.com
www.elinahelenius.com
Pages 6, 12ar, 84–89.

Gert Wingårdh – architect
Wingårdhs
Kungsgatan 10A
S-411 19 Göteborg
Sweden
T: + 46 (0)31 743 70 00
F: + 46 (0)31 711 98 38
wingardhs@wingardhs.se
www.wingardhs.se
Pages endpapers, 16r–17l, 23, 90–97.

Ilkka Suppanen
Studio Suppanen
Sturenkatu 13
00510 Helsinki
Finland
T: + 35 8 9 622 78737
F: + 35 8 9 622 3093
info@suppanen.com
www.suppanen.com
Pages 2,16l, 26–27, 128–33.

Ingegerd Raman
Bergsgafan 53
SE-11231 Stockholm
Sweden
T: + 46 8 6502824
F: + 46 8 660 7559
Ingegerd.raman@orrefors.se
Pages 3, 4–5, 22b, 25b, 122–27.

Lund Hagem Arkitekter AS
Filipstadun 5
0250 Oslo
Norway
T: + 47 23 33 31 50
F: + 47 22 01 69 01
mail@lundhagem.no
www.lundhagem.no
Pages 13b, 15al, 17r, 20b, 74–81, 108–15.

M2 A/S
Sibirien
Centralværkstedet
Værkmestergade 13
8000 Århus C
Denmark
T: + 45 70 23 24 23
F: + 45 86 15 70 71
info@m2.dk
Pages 18–19, 134–39.

Matti Sanaksenaho
Sanaksenaho Architects
Tehtaankatu 27–29D
00150 Helsinki
Finland
Pages 6, 12ar, 84–89.

Mikko Pulkkinen
Architect M.Sc, SAFA
Finland
mikko.pulkkinen@ark-lpr.fi
Pages 12al, 62–67.

NOD
Katarinavagen 17
116 45 Stockholm
Sweden
nod@natur-orienterad-design.se
www.natur-orienterad-design.se
Pages 90–97.

Peter Hulting
Meter Arkitektur
Kolonigatan 4
413 21 Göteborg
Sweden
T: + 46 31 204330
peter@meterarkitektur.se
www.meterarkitektur.se
Pages 11a, 15 b, 20–21a, 68–73.

Schmidt Hammer Lassen
Vester Farimagsgade 3
1606 Copenhagen v
Denmark
T: + 45 70 20 19 00
info@shl.dk
Pages 1, 12b, 19r, 24, 38–45, 116–21.

Tore.lindholm@nchr.uio.no
Pages 17ar, 20b, 74-81.

Woodnotes Oy
Tallberginkatu 1 B
00180 Helsinki
Finland
T: + 35 8 694 2200
F: + 35 8 694 2221
woodnotes@woodnotes.fi
www.woodnotes.fi
Pages 3 (inset), 7, 10b, 14, 15ar, 20l, 22al&r, 54–61.

INDEX

Page numbers in *italics* refer to captions.

ACKNOWLEDGMENTS

Magnus Englund and Chrystina Schmidt would like to thank all the staff at the Skandium office and shop, in particular Karl Lamberg for his efficient help with interviews and checking of Finnish spellings. We should also like to thank those of our suppliers who still inspire us to combine business with a greater design vision – not least Iittala, Marimekko, Woodnotes and Asplund. We should like to express our appreciation of the well-informed advice and generous support provided by Laura Sarvilinna and her team at Huippu Communications, the formidable trend, design and PR agency in Helsinki. Special thanks also go to Pål Lunder at Fjordfiesta for his invaluable guidance in finding exciting properties in Norway.

Magnus wishes to thank Chrystina's parents for introducing him to a genuine Finnish country house in the Åbo archipelago, and to his first wood-fired sauna. He would also like to thank his own parents, who have been buying far too many copies of *Scandinavian Modern* in the bookshops of Stockholm, and Ryland Peters & Small for twice trusting a Swede to write in English. Finally, but most importantly, many warm thanks to Christopher Seidenfaden for believing in Skandium through the years.